Lindsay Kaplan

ABOUT THE AUTHOR

ALEX IRVINE is the author of the novels *The Narrows; The Life of Riley; One King, One Soldier;* and *A Scattering of Jades.* His short fiction, published in *Salon, Vestal Review, The Magazine of Fantasy and Science Fiction, Trampoline,* and elsewhere, is collected in *Unintended Consequences* and *Pictures from an Expedition.* He has also written tie-in novels (*Batman: Inferno, The Ultimates: Against All Enemies*), comic books (*Hellstorm: Son of Satan*), and online narratives. He has won the Locus, Crawford, and IHG awards for his fiction, and has been nominated for the Pushcart Prize and the World Fantasy Award. His fiction has been translated into French, Spanish, Italian, Czech, Polish, Hebrew, Russian, and Chinese. In 2005, he was awarded the New England Press Association's top prize for investigative journalism, and that same year was part of a writing team that won a Webby and the International Game Developers Association Innovation Award. He is an assistant professor of English at the University of Maine.

THE
SUPERNATURAL™
BOOK
of
Monsters, Spirits,
Demons, and Ghouls

THE
SUPERNATURAL™
BOOK
of
Monsters, Spirits, Demons, and Ghouls

ALEX IRVINE

Illustrations by Dan Panosian
Supernatural created by Eric Kripke

TITAN BOOKS

Supernatural Book of Monsters, Demons, Spirits and Ghouls
ISBN: 9781848562790

Published by
Titan Books
A division of
Titan Publishing Group Ltd
144 Southwark Street
London
SE1 0UP

First UK edition April 2009
10 9 8 7 6 5 4 3 2

Part Opener & Chapter Opener art © istockphoto.com/blackred
Notebook Art © istockphoto.com/Royce Degrie

™ & © 2008 Warner Bros. Entertainment Inc. All rights reserved.

Designed by Jaime Putorti

Visit our website:
www.titanbooks.com

To receive advance information, news, competitions, and exclusive Titan offers online, please register as a member by clicking the "sign up" button on
our website: **www.titanbooks.com**
Did you enjoy this book? We love to hear from our readers. Please e-mail
us at: **readerfeedback@titanemail.com** or write to Reader Feedback at the
above address.

A CIP catalogue record for this title is available from the British Library.

Printed and bound in the UK by CPI Mackays, Chatham ME5 8TD

Contents

GHOULS, REVENANTS, ET CETERA

WITCHES, FAMILIARS, AND BLACK DOGS

DEMONS

Preface

From ghoulies and ghosties and long-legged beasties,
good Lord, preserve us.
—OLD IRISH SAYING

And when the good Lord won't, we will.
—NEWISH WINCHESTER SAYING

Sam and Dean Winchester, at your service. We're hunters. Dispatchers of spirits, scourges of the undead and unnatural, feared by demons and shapeshifters and boogeymen of all shapes and sizes. In a nutshell? We track down monsters, and then we blow the suckers away.

We've been in this line of work all our lives. Sam was six months old when a demon killed our mother. Dean was five years old. You might say we've both grown up in the family business. Neither one of us has ever held an honest job, except for Sam briefly while he was off deluding himself that he could lead a normal life. The murder of his girlfriend Jessica—in exactly the way our mother was murdered—put an end to that dream, and he rejoined the firm of Winchester and Sons.

Then, last year, the family business was cut back down to two. Our dad sacrificed himself to save Dean. Cut a deal with the same demonic bastard that killed our mother and killed Jessica. Now we're out to get that Yellow-Eyed Son of a Bitch, and we're taking down every evil thing we run across along the way.

We're not the only ones. You might not see them, or recognize their work, but there are other hunters out there. People who have dedicated their lives to keeping you safe from things you didn't know existed and wouldn't want to believe in if you did. Some of them taught our dad the ropes: Daniel Elkins, Bobby Singer—good people. And some of them have helped us along the way, like Jo and Ellen Harvelle.

And some of them have let hunting turn them into the kind of monster they spend their lives trying to snuff. Yeah, Gordon. We're talking to you.

It's a real problem. You look into the abyss, Nietzsche said, and the abyss looks back. Number one on the hunter's list of priorities is wasting evil, but number 1A is making sure that what you're about to waste really *is* evil. Sometimes it isn't easy. Sometimes all you have to go on is your gut instinct, and sometimes you make decisions that get people killed.

So how do you tell the difference between a haunt and a plain old run of bad luck? That's one of the questions that's plagued hunters from the beginning. Back in medieval Europe, people were a little more likely to jump to supernatural conclusions; now, we find all the time that a series of accidents that might look like a haunting or curse isn't anything of the kind. It's a rough old world out there, even without the demons and black magic and unquiet spirits.

Often enough, though, there are things that can't be explained by science, or even by the various weird extremes of human behavior. We've learned to distinguish the supernatural from the merely bizarre.

Our dad taught us to look for patterns. If there's a string of unexplained deaths in a particular place, has it happened before? Some supernatural bad guys appear for a few years, or a few days, and then disappear for a while. *Shtrigas* are like that, and *rakshasas*, and some kinds of demons. Some angry spirits work along the same pattern. They take out their frustrations for a while and then lie low, which makes it harder sometimes to figure out what's got them so riled up. Hard to waste a spirit when you don't know what's motivating it. Know thine enemy, it says somewhere; our dad drilled that into us, too.

Some patterns are easy to figure. Killings on the full moon? Fits the MO of a werewolf—although it's not always that simple. Series of drownings, year after year, near the summer solstice? We'll put our money on a *nix*. Mass disappearances near a certain location? Angry spirit, details TK. Strange weather patterns and localized crop failures? That one's probably a demon—more later on that. Much more.

Other patterns might include a relationship among all of the people affected. Do they hang out at the same bar? Did they all play baseball on the same Little League team? Have they all owned, at one time or another, a particular item that might be carrying a curse? This part of the job is just like police work. The difference is that cops put criminals in jail. We put spirits back in the afterlife, and demons back in hell.

In this book, we're going to take you through the various spirits and monsters and demons that we've run into while searching for the big one: the Yellow-Eyed Demon that destroyed our family. There's a war coming, and when it starts, we're all going to need to know as much as we can about the other side.

So read on, and see what it's like when you take a step into the world of the supernatural.

THE
SUPERNATURAL™
BOOK
of
Monsters, Spirits,
Demons, and Ghouls

SPIRITS

Spirits come in all kinds, and they can be provoked to stay in the world of the living by any kind of emotion: love or hate, sadness or confusion. Dad quotes the English demonologist Ebenezer Sibly in his journals:

> In the world of spirits is always a very great number of them, as being the first sort of all, in order to their examination and preparation; but there is no fixed time for their stay; for some are translated to heaven and others confined to hell soon after their arrival; whilst some continue there for weeks, and others for several years.

Almost always, a spirit is tied to a material object. More often than not, that material object is the spirit's own remains. We spend a lot of time digging up bones. But we've also worked jobs where the spirit was residing in jewelry, dolls, picture frames, you name it. In a nutshell, here's what we've learned:

Anything can be haunted.

After death, some spirits don't want to go. They think their work on earth isn't done, or they feel they have to right some wrong or avenge some injustice. So they don't go. They hang around the material world, unable to touch anything or talk to anyone, and their only company is other spirits as lost and confused as they are. It doesn't take Dr. Phil to figure out that eventually all of that feeling is going to turn bad.

When it does, you've got a spirit that might be evil, or might be angry, or might just be lashing out from pure anguish. Whatever the reasons, these spirits tend to be fatal to the people who get in their way, and it's our job to see them back on their path to the after-life.

Dispelling a spirit is pretty straightforward, even though it's not always easy. You find the remains, or the object the spirit is using as a focus to stay active in the human world. When you've found it, you salt it and burn it. End of spirit. Maybe it lacks a little finesse,

but it gets the job done. Sometimes you can even get away with just giving the body a proper burial. That works if the spirit hasn't had time to go crazy in the limbo between this world and the next. And if it turns out to be a death omen—well, they're satisfied just to be noticed.

Here's an old story, maybe one of the oldest, about a spirit like that. It's one of Dad's favorites—well, *was* one of Dad's favorites. It's maybe *the* prototype haunted-house story.

PLINY THE YOUNGER, LETTER TO SURA:

There was at Athens a large and roomy house, which had a bad name, so that no one could live there. In the dead of the night a noise, resembling the clashing of iron, was frequently heard, which, if you listened more attentively, sounded like the rattling of chains, distant at first, but approaching nearer by degrees: immediately afterward a specter appeared in the form of an old man, of extremely emaciated and squalid appearance, with a long beard and disheveled hair, rattling the chains on his feet and hands. The distressed occupants meanwhile passed their wakeful nights under the most dreadful terrors imaginable. This, as it broke their rest, ruined their health, and brought on distempers, their terror grew upon them, and death ensued. Even in the daytime, though the spirit did not appear, yet the impression remained so strong upon their imaginations that it still seemed before their eyes, and kept them in perpetual alarm. Consequently the house was at length deserted, as being deemed absolutely uninhabitable; so that it was now entirely abandoned to the ghost. However, in hopes that some tenant might be found who was ignorant of this very alarming circumstance, a bill was put up, giving notice that it was either to be let or sold. It happened that Athenodorus the philosopher came to Athens at this time, and, reading the bill, enquired the price. The extraordinary cheapness raised his suspicion; nevertheless, when he heard the whole story, he was so far from being discouraged that he was more strongly inclined to hire it, and, in short, actually did so. When it grew toward evening, he ordered a couch to be prepared for him in the front part of the house, and, after calling for a light, together with his pencil and tablets, directed all his people to retire. But that his mind might not, for want of employment, be open to the vain terrors of imaginary noises and spirits, he applied himself to writing with the utmost attention. The first part of the night passed in entire silence, as usual; at length a clanking of iron and rattling of chains was heard: however, he neither lifted up his eyes nor laid down his pen, but in order to keep calm and collected, tried to pass the sounds off to himself as something else. The noise increased and advanced nearer, till it seemed at the door, and at last in the chamber. He looked up, saw, and recognized the ghost exactly as it had been described to him: it stood before him, beckoning with a finger, like a person who calls another. Athenodorus in reply made a sign with his hand that it should wait a little, and threw his eyes again upon his papers; the ghost then rattled its chains over the head of the philosopher, who looked upon this, and seeing it beckoning as before, immediately arose, and, light in hand, followed it. The ghost slowly stalked along, as if encumbered with its chains, and, turning into the area of the house, suddenly vanished. Athenodorus, being thus deserted, made a mark with some grass and leaves on the spot where the spirit left him. The next day he gave information to the magistrates, and advised them to order that spot to be dug up. This was accordingly done, and the skeleton of a man in chains was found there; for the body, having lain a considerable time in the ground, was putrefied and mouldered away from the fetters. The bones, being collected together, were publicly buried, and thus after the ghost was appeased by the proper ceremonies, the house was haunted no more.

So that explains why reburial will work, at least sometimes. Why salt, though? Folklore about our favorite mineral compound goes back thousands of years, and it's always represented purity. The Greeks, Romans, and Hebrews all sacrificed it, considered it powerful—and ate a lot of it. The Romans even salted their wine. We've known hunters who salt their beer—this comes from an old Scottish tradition in which a pinch of salt was added to a batch of mash to keep witches out of it. Romanian legend has it that pregnant women who don't eat salt will give birth to vampires. In Japanese folklore, troublesome ghosts are packed in jars of salt. Salt also symbolizes permanence, and the Old Testament refers to the "covenant of salt" between Yahweh and his wayward children. Scot's *Discoverie of Witchcraft*, from 1584, tells us that "the Devil loveth no salt in his meat."

And spirits loveth no salt blasted out of the barrel of a gun into their ectoplasmic mugs. It doesn't kill them, but it does get them out of your way for a while. It might also keep them out of your house if you place it along doorways and windowsills, but we've never seen that work for long.

Another trick we learned along the way is that most spirits and witches don't like iron. Our father had a theory that iron's magnetism has something to do with its power. We'll go along with that, but the important thing to us is that it works. And we're part of a long tradition of using it. Irish mothers used to put iron in their babies' cribs to prevent fairies or elves from switching the baby for a changeling; it's part of the bedrock of European folklore that witches can't pass over cold iron—and this one is true. We've seen it work. The Greeks and Romans kept iron out of their temples and cemeteries because they wanted spirits around and knew that iron would chase them away (the flip side of this is the iron fences around cemeteries, there to keep ghosts in). Cold iron—iron that isn't smelted out of ore, but hammered pure without heating—is best, but any iron will do in a pinch.

Although there are some rules—spirits don't like iron, and they don't like salt, and they usually don't like us—beyond that, every spirit is a little different. Oh—also, they tend to smell of ozone, for reasons that we still haven't figured out. Here are some of the bad mofos we've run into over the past couple of years.

The Woman in White

This one appears all over the world, and keeps coming. We've taken care of maybe a dozen of them since we were kids. The basic story goes like this:

A young woman, in a despairing fury over her treatment at the hands of her husband, murders her children. Or she kills them because they prevent her from marrying the man of her dreams. In either case, she then dies and becomes a spirit. The most famous version is probably the Mexican one:

Long ago, the story goes, a beautiful Indian princess, Doña Luisa de Loveros, fell in love with a handsome Mexican nobleman named Don Nuno de Montesclaros. The princess loved the nobleman deeply and had two children by him, but Montesclaros refused to marry her. When he finally deserted her and married another woman, Doña Luisa went mad with rage and stabbed her two children. Authorities found her wandering the street, sobbing, her clothes covered in blood. They charged her with infanticide and sent her to the gallows.

Ever since, it is said, the ghost of La Llorona ("the crying woman") walks the country at night in her bloody dress, crying out for her murdered children. If she finds any child, she's likely to carry it away with her to the nether regions, where her own spirit dwells.

Even this is a newer version of a much older story, maybe all the way back to when the conquistadores were doing their thing along the Rio Grande—which just goes to show you how long these kinds of spirits have been around. There's another version from a little closer to home, recorded outside Dallas. In this one, known as the Ghost of White Rock Lake, La Llorona comes together with a famous urban legend, the vanishing hitchhiker. In this one, a driver (almost always at night) picks up a hitchhiker, who then either disappears as the car passes a graveyard or gives an address that turns out to be a long-abandoned house. Our father had some pretty definite ideas about the vanishing hitchhiker:

> Always dangerous because it preys on one of the best human qualities, the impulse to help those in need. The problem with the vanishing hitchhiker is that it never stays vanished. It leaves a token sometimes, which leads the person who offered the ride to try to find it again. Usually that search leads straight to a graveyard, and there's one less Good Samaritan in the world. Some spirits know they can't approach directly, and some just love the game of taking advantage of the better side of human nature.

Around White Rock Lake, you'll see strange lights, hear strange noises, and the locals will probably tell you a story if you stick around long enough to hear it. There's the pretty girl in a white evening dress, soaking wet, who flags down a ride and then disappears before the car gets to the address she gives. There's the same girl, showing up on the porches of lakeside houses asking to use the phone and then vanishing, leaving only a puddle of water and the fading echoes of her screams.

We've heard of other La Llorona cases in Bachelor's Grove Cemetery, Chicago; Fort Monroe, Virginia; Cry-Woman's Bridge in Dublin, Indiana; Calumet Bridge in Gary, Indiana—something about Chicagoland seems to draw them like flies. But we've heard of woman in white/vanishing hitchhiker legends from as far away as Singapore. Those are the harmless ones. The ones we haven't had to take care of yet because either they're just wandering spirits or they haven't gotten around to turning malevolent yet.

The last time we dealt with a woman in white was in Jericho, California, a couple of years ago. Like the White Rock Lake ghost, she was a vanishing hitchhiker. She'd ask for a ride home, and if you gave her one, you found yourself at an old abandoned house out in the middle of nowhere, and you weren't going to have to worry about getting home. Also, in this case, the spirit—Constance Welch—was a suicide. She'd drowned her kids and then jumped off Sylvania Bridge. Sometimes suicides turn into angry spirits who aren't focused on the people who did them wrong in real life. They're just lost and hurting, and over time that turns dark, and they start going after anyone who vaguely resembles the people who might have driven them to suicide.

Our dad, after taking out a WiW outside Durant, Oklahoma, in 1991, wrote in his journal that he thought La Llorona was the same kind of spirit the Irish called a *bean sidhe*, or

> Banshee. Sometimes they are dressed in white, sometimes in a winding sheet or burial gown. They wail, they scream, sometimes they sing to signal that death approaches for some member of the household where they are heard. Usually they come in one of three forms, which correspond to the three stages of womanhood (and maybe have something to do with the age of the person whose death is being signaled). A banshee is either a beautiful young woman, a matron, or a corpselike hag. As a hag, she has a link, way back, with notorious English hag figures such as Black Annis, a one-eyed crone, physically strong and with the features of a demon: long teeth, iron claws, and a blue face. She was said to hide in a giant oak that was the sole survivor of the primeval forest. Like many hag figures, she was a cannibal who

preferred children, which she ate after flaying them alive. Their skins hung in a cave beneath the tree.

Baba Yaga, from Russian lore, is another example. Living deep in the forest, in a magical hut that moved around on chicken legs, she often ate children, but unlike Black Annis, Baba Yaga could be an important source of magical help for a hero or questing child. If you asked her the right kind of question, or caught her in the right mood, she might help you on your errand instead of making a meal of you.

The banshee often appears crying as she washes bloody clothes by a river—usually the clothes of someone about to die. Also, she can appear as a crow, rabbit, or weasel.

The banshee is more of an omen spirit than the woman in white tends to be, but the relationship is there. At least in the Jericho case, seeing Constance Welch was a sure sign that you were going to die.

Water Spirits

Women in white throwing themselves into rivers, banshees washing bloody clothing on a riverbank—spirits love water. Some of them are always found there. The Sirens of the *Odyssey* are probably the most famous water spirits in history, but they weren't the only ones. The Slavic countries have their *vodyanoy* and *rusalka*, the Native Americans had *mannegishi*, the Germans had the Lorelei, the British Isles had more water spirits than you could shake a stick at: kelpies and nymphs and the *each uisge*. They tend to pop up in the United States wherever there are immigrant populations that make them feel at home.

Our father tangled with a long list of water spirits and left some notes about them in his journal.

VODYANOY. Russian male water spirit, sometimes said to be a shapeshifter but more often appears as an old man, skin freckled with scales, a green beard tangled with muck and underwater plants. May live in whirlpools. In larger bodies of water, often lives in sunken ships, served by the ghosts of the ships' drowned crews. Drowns people to serve him as slaves, but also protects fishermen who appease him by giving him the first fish of their catch. Likes butter and tobacco.

Also likes the RUSALKA, and often either marries one or takes several as servants/concubines. RUSALKI are spirits of women who are murdered or die by suicide in water—sometimes children who were drowned by their mothers. (See WOMAN IN WHITE.) The adult versions sing to seduce passersby or sailors, then draw them underwater to become their spirit lovers. Lore sometimes suggests vampiric qualities. Some RUSALKI will vanish if their deaths are avenged. Can also be dispelled if kept out of water long enough for her hair to dry completely. The child versions can be dispelled by baptism with holy water.

Have heard of VODYANOY from hunters in Alaska. Never seen one.

The Germanic NIX combines attributes of the VODYANOY and the RUSALKA. In human form, the NIX is usually male and handsome and dangerous to unmarried women and unbaptized children. Most active at summer and winter solstice (Christianized versions of the legend say Christmas Eve). Plays music to beguile its target. Also an omen of drowning—similar to a banshee—and can be heard screaming from the water, signaling that someone is going to drown there. Like the VODYANOY, the NIX likes tobacco, and also vodka. Can be made to appear by dripping blood into water, or by sacrificing a black animal.

Once, in Pinckney, Michigan, I suckered a NIX by using a Black Shuck as the sacrifice. That was a show, a demon dog tangling with a water spirit. The Shuck won, and I sent it back to hell for its trouble.

Sometimes the NIX appears as a horse called Bäckahästen that if ridden will leap into the nearest body of water, drowning the rider. Overlap here with Celtic/Scottish stories of the kelpie and EACH UISGE. Kelpies appear from the fog near rivers, and if ridden drown their riders. The EACH UISGE can be ridden safely as long as it can't see or smell water. The minute it does, it drags the rider in and devours him, leaving only the liver.

This last detail I thought was just storyteller's elaboration until I tangled with an EACH UISGE at the Quabbin Reservoir in Massachusetts. That one took human form, too, and looked like a handsome young man who always had weeds in his hair. I was lucky to get out with my liver.

I used to like swimming, but that's one more thing I lost to the job.

Water spirits don't need much water, either. See British legends of Jenny Greenteeth or Peg-o'-the-Well.

MANNEGISHI, Native American spirits living in rapids, like to play jokes on humans, and the jokes tend to turn deadly. One of their favorites is to tip canoes in rapids. I tracked a MANNEGISHI down in Minnesota, not far from Pastor Jim's. It got seven kayakers before I got it.

We've done a little scuba-spirit hunting of our own. Something about water, about drowning, makes for angry spirits. There's the Chinese *nisigui*, or water ghost—we like to call 'em scapeghosts. In Chinese tradition, people who have drowned can't be reincarnated. So what do they do? Get someone else to drown, which frees them to move on. A scapeghost. There was a series of scapeghost drownings in Boston's Fort Point Channel a few years back. And Japanese folklore is full of ghosts with long, wet hair.

But just as often, a water spirit is just a spirit whose body died in water. It hangs around for the same reasons spirits always do: to be avenged, or because it just can't stand to go. Couple years back, we ran into one in Lake Manitoc, Wisconsin. Over thirty-five years or so, it killed more than a half-dozen people, and when we got to the bottom of it, we found a scared kid. His two older friends were bullying him one day, and it got out of hand and he drowned. So he kept coming back, and he stripped his two friends of all the people they loved, until the second friend—who happened to be the sheriff of the town, so you can imagine how tricky it was to get all this figured out—sacrificed himself to save his grandson. That was one of the tough ones.

Urban Legends and Vengeful Spirits

You've all heard the one about the hook man, right? A guy and a girl making out, they hear on the radio that a deranged killer is on the loose, recognizable because he's got a hook for a hand. The girl gets spooked and says she wants to go home. Here's where the story goes in two directions. If the guy goes along with it, if he's gallant and takes her home, they arrive at the girl's house—to find a hook prosthesis dangling from one of the door handles.

If the guy doesn't go along with it, if he decides he'll just take a

look around outside to settle the girl's nerves so they can get back to business, then a short time later the girl hears a strange scraping sound on the roof of the car. She gets up her nerve, looks outside—and finds her boyfriend dead, hanging from a tree over the car. The scraping sound is the boyfriend's fingernails on the roof.

That's a nice little cautionary tale against trying for second base after the movie, right? Well, sometimes spirits use our stories to give them form. There are some real, nonsupernatural stories about killers stalking lovers' lanes—anyone ever hear of the Son of Sam? And remember how he swore he saw a black dog telling him to kill? More about black dogs later . . .

Before the Son of Sam, right after World War II, there was a lovers' lane killer in Arkansas. Since then, we've read about cases in Los Angeles; Norman; Oklahoma; all over the place. Some of them we've looked into and found a vengeful spirit who's a little too hung up on teenage chastity.

Once we actually ran into a hook man. A killer with a big nasty hook for a hand. He put on a big show of morality and then went out at night and killed whoever he'd decided was immoral. Prostitutes, mostly, since they were easy targets. His evil persisted after his death, even after his hook had been melted down and recast into—of all things—a necklace given by a father to his daughter. The father was a pastor who didn't always practice what he preached, if you get our drift, and his daughter's troubled mind brought the hook man back through her necklace. Classic haunted object, classic vengeful spirit.

Here's another classic. You stand in front of a mirror in a dark room and say "Bloody Mary." Either three times, or thirteen times, or a hundred times. Maybe you do it at midnight, maybe you have a lit candle, maybe you spin around in circles, maybe you do it while walking up a stairway backward.

Who's Bloody Mary? The name comes from England's Queen

Mary Tudor, who was notorious for her persecution of Protestant dissenters. But it's been applied to a lot of people since then. Mary Worth, for example, accused and convicted of killing her children—but nobody is sure where or when. Probably in your town, a long time ago. Or Bloody Mary can be the ghost of a woman murdered right after her wedding, who might have been pregnant, and you can summon her by saying you killed her baby. If you do it, the story goes, and Mary appears, one of two things can happen. Either she's going to tell you something about your future, or she's going to tear your face off and kill you.

The mirror part of the story goes back a long way, farther back than most people probably know. Here's what Dad said about it:

SUPERNATURAL Book of Monsters, Spirits, Demons, and Ghouls

Divination by mirror has been practiced in nearly all cultures for as long as mirrors have been around. Before that, any reflective surface, especially still water, was used to prophesy or catch a glimpse of the future. Aztecs created TEZCATLIPOCA, "smoking mirrors," out of mercury poured into a bowl. Queen Elizabeth I's court magician, John Dee, prophesied with mirrors. Folklore from various places holds that if you perform a certain ritual while looking in a mirror—eating an apple, brushing your hair, conducting any one of a thousand "wise woman" domestic rituals—you will see your future husband. A variation on this is looking into a well at sunrise to watch what reflection emerges as the light starts to shine into the well. In many of these stories, the danger is that you might also see the Grim Reaper, which means you will die before marrying.

Tradition also holds that at the moment of a death, all of the mirrors in a house should be covered so they don't trap the departing spirit.

It's bad luck to break mirrors because they're reflections of the soul, but also because they hold the future. That's why the seven years of bad luck: you've broken your future.

And that's why there's a mirror involved in the Bloody Mary story. Anyway, if you're a girl, chances are you were at a slumber party once and someone dared you to summon Bloody Mary. Or maybe it hasn't happened yet, but believe us, it will.

Here's our advice: *Don't.* She might show up.

How do we know?

Because we've met her. Or maybe we should say that we met a

spirit that used the Bloody Mary urban legend as a way to get itself back into the material world. We tracked down a ghost, eventually, of a murdered girl named Mary Worthington. Her killer cut out her eyes, and her spirit occupied a mirror in the house where she died. As she died, she tried to write her killer's name on the wall, but she never finished it, and the secret died with her. Wherever that mirror went, she went, and whenever someone summoned her in that place, she came to life—well, "life"—and killed the summoner if he or she had a dark secret.

That's how spirits work. They sort of lose their ability to think in shades of gray after a while.

Truth is, we're kind of like that, too. Comes with the territory. Doesn't matter how spirits get dangerous, whether they were evil or they just turned crazy from being stuck between two worlds. There's black, and then there's white. When spirits start hurting people, we take them out.

Land Spirits: Native and Immigrant

▶ NATIVE AMERICAN CURSES

The old Indian burial ground curse is enough of a chestnut that the first time we ran into one, even *we* couldn't believe it. I mean, when you consider all of the weird stuff we've seen that we'd never heard of before, to suddenly stumble across the oldest of the old radio-serial kind of haunting—kind of jarring.

But American history is chock-full of Native American curses that seem to be bearing fruit, and us Euro-Americans have been talking about Native American ghosts practically since we arrived at Plymouth Rock. Here's one example, from a poem written in 1787 by some guy we'd never heard of named Philip Freneau:

THE INDIAN BURYING GROUND

In spite of all the learned have said,
I still my old opinion keep;
The posture that we give the dead,
Points out the soul's eternal sleep.

Not so the ancients of these lands—
The Indian, when from life released,

Again is seated with his friends,
And shares again the joyous feast.

His imaged birds, and painted bowl,
And venison, for a journey dressed,
Bespeak the nature of the soul,
Activity, that knows no rest.

His bow, for action ready bent,
And arrows, with a head of bone,
Can only mean that life is spent,
And not the finer essence gone.

Thou, stranger, that shalt come this way,
No fraud upon the dead commit,
Yet, marking the swelling turf, and say,
They do not lie, but here they sit.

Here, still a lofty rock remains,
On which the curious eye may trace
(Now wasted half by wearing rains)
The fancies of a ruder race.

Here, still an aged elm aspires,
Beneath whose far-projecting shade
(And which the shepherd still admires)
The children of the forest played.

There oft a restless Indian queen,
(Pale Marian, with her braided hair)
And many a barbarous form is seen
To chide the man that lingers there.

By midnight moons, o'er moistening dews,
In habit for the chase arrayed,
The hunter still the deer pursues,
The hunter and the deer—a shade.

And long shall timorous fancy see
The painted chief, and pointed spear,
And reason's self shall bow the knee
To shadows and delusions here.

"Activity that knows no rest" is right. If there's one thing that can give the Energizer Bunny a run for its money persistence-wise, that one thing would be an Indian curse.

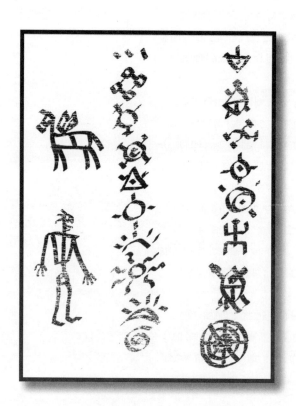

▶ AMITYVILLE

In 1644, relations between the English and the Dutch on what is now Long Island, New York, were touchy, and one of the problems was that the two parties couldn't agree on how to treat the local Massapequa Indians, whose chief Tackapausha claimed that he had sold the Dutch only the use of the land their settlements occupied—not the land itself. After going back and forth about the problem, the Dutch decided to take matters into their own hands, hiring a certain Captain John Underhill, a feared Indian fighter who during the Pequot War a few years before had become known for the Mystic massacre, in which four hundred Pequots were burned alive or slaughtered as they fled a village near the Mystic River. With this atrocity on his resume, and having recently moved to the island of Manhattan (his plot of land is now the site of Trinity Church), he was the perfect person for the Dutch to hire to remove their Massapequa problem. This he did, first presiding over the torture and killing of seven Massapequa accused of stealing pigs, and then ambushing and slaughtering approximately 120 Massapequa and burying them in a mass grave at a site known as Fort Neck. For this, and another massacre conducted a few months later in what is now Westchester County, he earned a fee of twenty-five thousand Dutch guilders.

When a road was built on the Fort Neck site, years later, the soil was said to be redder than anywhere else in the area. An archeological dig on the presumed site, near the time of the road construction, uncovered the bones of twenty-four people, presumably some of Underhill's Massapequa victims. The rest have never been found.

What's interesting about this is that the Fort Neck site is about a mile from 112 Ocean Avenue, the address of probably the most famous haunting in American history. After Butch DeFeo killed his parents and four siblings in the house, he claimed to have been possessed by the spirit of an Indian chief while committing the murders. The Lutzes, the next family that lived there, fled after less than a month, driven away by an avalanche of paranormal activity. You've seen the movie: sulfurous smells coming from the "red room" in the basement, temperature fluctuations, a crucifix turning upside down, ectoplasmic oozings from the walls—classic poltergeist. Wouldn't surprise us a bit if Tackapausha or one of the other Massapequa who died at Fort Neck was just angry enough, and died just violently enough, to coalesce into that kind of angry spirit.

Some of the Lutzes' story has been questioned, but we know it's not unusual for people who have experienced the supernatural to have unclear or fragmentary recollections of it. People also make stuff up. But hey, if you ask us, a local history of massacred Indians and mass graves is more than enough to spur a haunting. Could be the Lutzes got off easy.

▶ ROUTE 55

There are plenty of other examples, some of them not as spectacular—but definitely more lethal—than Amityville. Take the case of New Jersey Route 55, which was rebuilt through Deptford in the spring of 1983. A local Delaware Indian—either Carl Pierce or Sachem Wayandaga, depending on where you see him quoted—warned state planners that their proposed path for the road violated one of the local burial grounds of the tribe. But, being state bureaucrats, they didn't pay any attention.

According to the Newark *Star-Ledger*, the following accidents befell the project:

- A worker was run over by a steamroller
- A worker died when he was blown off an overpass by freak high winds
- An inspector keeled over on-site from a brain aneurysm
- A van carrying transportation department workers to the site blew up

Off-site, during the first week of construction, four family members of project workers died unexpectedly. All for a seven-mile stretch of road.

The moral here is that when the local Indians tell you not to build a road, maybe you should listen.

▶ WISCONSIN LAKES CURSE—OH, AND THE BUGS

Here's one that Dad noted in his journal. We ran across it while trying to figure out what was going on in Oasis Plains, Oklahoma:

WISCONSIN LAKES CURSE

The last Indian who left Lake Wingra (sometimes known as Dead Lake) said that the lake would die. Over the next fifty years, the lake shrunk dramatically, and as the WISCONSIN STATE JOURNAL noted in 1923, "has also become noted for its hidden whirlpools, and for its treachery."

A Winnebago Indian was murdered on Maple Bluff

overlooking Lake Mendota. He called upon the lake spirits to curse the white settlers and kill two of them every year. From the same JOURNAL article: "Although this story is a fable, it is nevertheless true that scarcely a year has passed in the history of Madison, but that two whites have drowned in Mendota."

some fable.

Not that this has anything to do with Oasis Plains, but it's too good to pass up. And what did happen in Oasis Plains was strange enough that we wanted to take our time getting to it.

It was a subdivision like any other subdivision, filled with cookie-cutter McMansions that either one of us would chew a leg off to get out of if we lived there. Not that we're judgmental. While they were still building it out, a gas-company worker named Dustin Burwash fell into a sinkhole. By the time his coworker got to the hole and let a rope down, Dustin was dead, and his brain had turned to mush. The coroner called it mad-cow disease, but we've never known a coroner yet who could recognize the telltale signs of a supernatural murder. Takes a professional to do that.

We go looking around the development and meet Larry Pike, one of these self-appointed real-estate visionaries, always going on about how his magnificent cul-de-sacs rose from the wasteland of scrub, and then Larry's son Matt. Typical disaffected teenager, Matt, except he's got a thing for insects. And spiders. The same day, we find out that one of Larry's surveyors had been stung to death by bees the year before—and the next morning, another Realtor in the development buys it in the shower. Killed by spiders.

Right away we think we have this one solved. Obviously it's Matt, right? He's your prototypical vector for a vengeful spirit: an adolescent, unhappy with his family life, interested in stuff that most people think is weird.

Then we find out it's not that simple. Turns out Matt's been monitoring bug populations in the remaining prairie around Zombie Acres, or whatever the development is called—and they're going through the roof. He shows us one example, where the ground is literally roiling with earthworms. It's strange, for sure, but what's underneath is even stranger.

Hundreds of bones, buried in a mass grave.

Serial killer or Indian massacre, those are about the only options. And once we track down Jo White Tree at a reservation down the road, we find out which one. She told us this:

> Two hundred years ago, a band of my ancestors lived in that valley. One day the American cavalry came to relocate them. They were resistant, the cavalry impatient. As my grandfather put it, "On the night the moon and the sun share the sky as equals," the cavalry first raided our village. They murdered, raped. The next day, they came again. And the next and the next. On the sixth night, the cavalry came one last time. By the time the sun rose, every man, woman, and child still in the village was dead.

They say on the sixth night, as the chief of the village lay dying, he whispered to the heavens that no white man would ever tarnish this land again. Nature itself would rise up and protect the valley. And it would bring as many days of misery and death upon the white man as the cavalry had brought upon his people. And on the night of the sixth day, none would survive.

From there, we put it together. Dustin Burwash had died on the spring equinox, when "the sun and the moon share the sky as equals." The only guy on the land the previous spring equinox—the unlucky surveyor—didn't make it either.

And we found this out on the fourth day.

That was a long night. We couldn't convince Larry the McMansion King to leave, even though he and his family were the only people left after the other Realtor's spider problem. So we got to the house just as every bug in Oklahoma descended. Through some combination of luck and plain old dogged refusal to quit, we survived, and we kept the Pikes alive, too.

This one had at least a partially happy ending: Larry finally saw the light. Last time we saw him, he was swearing nobody would ever live on that land if he could help it.

So what happens if you get wind of an Indian curse and don't move? You can't break a curse, you can only get out of its way or try to weather it. Back in the 1700s in Illinois, a town tried to weather one. Ever heard of Kaskaskia? Of course you haven't. Here's why.

▶ CURSE OF KASKASKIA

Back in 1735, Kaskaskia was a center of Mississippi River commerce, with a large population of French settlers. A rich fur trader by the name of Bernard ran a trading post on the outskirts of town, and even though he didn't like the local Indians much, he hired them to do the menial work around the post. Turns out that one of these Indians had been educated by French missionaries, and Bernard, against all of his instincts, started to take a shine to him. Typical Frenchman, thinking anything is improved by contact with something French.

Problems arose when Bernard's daughter, Marie—the apple of his eye, since his wife wasn't around anymore—also started to take a shine to this Indian.

Real problems arose when Bernard figured out that the Indian felt the same way.

Well, it was one thing to enjoy having the Indian around to work for him, and something entirely different to contemplate his little white princess being defiled by the touch of a red man. Bernard canned the Indian and made sure he was blacklisted around town. Nobody in Kaskaskia would give him work. Eventually, he left town, but not before promising Marie that he would be back to claim her.

A year later, after Marie had withstood the courtships of several of the local French young men about town, a group of Indians passed through Kaskaskia. Among them, and keeping himself disguised to avoid trouble, was Marie's loverboy. They got together and headed north, out of Kaskaskia and away from Bernard.

This really set Bernard off, and he got together a posse and charged off after them, eventually running the pair to ground near Cahokia. Unhinged by this point, Bernard ordered his trapper cronies to tie the Indian to a log and set him adrift to drown in the Mississippi. Over Marie's protests they did, and before the Indian died, he swore a curse.

Before the year was out, he said, Bernard would be dead, and he and Marie would be together forever. Kaskaskia and all of its land would be ruined, its churches and houses destroyed, and its dead turned out of their graves.

Fast forward a year. Marie died, and Bernard challenged a business partner to a duel. One pistol shot later he was dead, too.

Over the next hundred years, as the river's channels shifted, Kaskaskia suffered so many floods that it became cut off from the mainland. People began to abandon the town, and it slowly died. It wasn't until 1973 that the church and altar were flooded and destroyed; long before that, the cemetery had been washed away and all the bodies lost to the river.

You can still find Kaskaskia on a map, but as of the last census, its population was—guess.

Nine.

Nine people, in a place that was the first state capital of Illinois.

That is why you don't mess with curses. You just get out of the way.

Vanir

Once in a while, we run into a town that's a little too Stepfordy, if you catch our drift. Lawns are perfect, people are real nice, gas is cheaper than anywhere else within twenty miles. It's spooky. Usually there's a good reason for that feeling of spookiness. We have yet to come across a place where everything is swell all the time without something being rotten underneath.

So one day we got a phone call from Dad, no big deal.

Ha. Joke there. It was the first time we'd heard from him in months, after he'd gone missing and we'd driven all over the country looking for him, so it was more like HOLY CRAP, WE GOT A PHONE CALL FROM DAD! AND HE TOLD US HE WAS ON THE TRAIL OF THE DEMON THAT KILLED MOM AND JESSICA!

And then he told us to go to Indiana. Even though *he* was in California.

Sometimes it's not easy being good sons, but we did it. Instead of joining the hunt for the Demon, we went to Burkittsville, Indiana, where for three consecutive years a couple had gone missing during the second week of April. Bo-ring.

Except it didn't turn out to be all that boring, because it turned out that the good people of Burkittsville were harboring a Norse god in their midst, and that in return for the kind of benefits you might expect from that kind of protection, they were sacrificing a male-and-female couple every year. In the second week of April.

Which was exactly when we rolled into town.

The Norse gods are basically divided into a couple of groups. Odin and Thor and all the biggies are the Aesir, who live in Asgard on the other side of the Rainbow Bridge. Then there are the Vanir, who live in a place called Vanaheim. The Vanir are the Aesir's scruffy opposite numbers, the wild children, worshiped for their protection of nature and for their help with fertility. They can bring health, luck, wealth, and so forth—if they are given the right kind of sacrifices.

Some of the rituals that go along with this kind of stuff are pretty interesting. The Roman historian Tacitus, in *Germania*, recorded a sacrifice to the Vanir known as Nerthus:

> On an island in the sea stands an inviolate grove, in which, veiled with a cloth, is a chariot that none but the priest may touch. The priest can feel the presence of the goddess in this holy of holies, and attends her with deepest reverence as her chariot is drawn along by cows. Then follow days of rejoicing and merrymaking in every place that she condescends to visit and sojourn in. No one goes to war, no one takes up arms; every iron object is locked away. . . . After that, the chariot, the vestments, and (believe it if you will) the goddess herself are cleansed in a secluded lake. This service is performed by slaves who are immediately afterward drowned in the lake.

Historians and archeologists have also dug up all kinds of bodies from peat bogs in Denmark and the British Isles that bear marks of ritual sacrifice. And there are other stories, too. The Germanic tribes did quite a bit of sacrificing, some of it recorded by Adam of Bremen, who wrote about a ceremony in Uppsala:

> The sacrifice is as follows: of every living creature they offer nine head, and with the blood of those it is the custom to placate the gods, but the bodies are hanged in a grove which is near the temple; so holy is that grove to the heathens that each tree in it is presumed to be divine by reason of the victim's

death and putrefaction. There also dogs and horses hang along with men. One of the Christians told me that he had seen seventy-two bodies of various kinds hanging there, but the incantations which are usually sung at this kind of sacrifice are various and disgraceful, and so we had better say nothing about them.

In Sweden, even kings could be sacrificed, and at least two of them—Olof Trätälja and Domalde—were, after years of famine. Domalde had it easy. His retainers just cut him up and sprinkled his blood on an altar. Olof went the hard way. His people accused him of shirking sacrifices, and when he didn't straighten up fast enough for them, they surrounded his house and burned him inside it.

The Greek historian Strabo wrote about human sacrifice among the Cymri, who hung prisoners taken during a battle over bronze bowls before priestesses cut their throats. The priestesses performed divinations from the flow of blood into the bowls, and from this predicted the outcome of the battle. Strabo also mentions the Wicker Man sacrifices, in which a "colossus of straw and wood" was filled with wild animals, livestock, and humans before being burned. Julius Caesar, in his memoir of the Gallic Wars, described the Wicker Man as "with limbs woven out of twigs, filled with living

men and set on fire so that the victims perished in a sheet of flame."

And then there are the Aztecs, who genuinely believed that if they didn't keep the blood flowing on their altars, the world would stop existing. Enough said.

That wasn't how they did things in Burkittsville. Their Vanir took the form of a scarecrow, which isn't a big jump, since scarecrow-like effigies were common in pagan Europe. Depending on the source you look at, the scarecrow was either a later replacement for an actual human sacrifice conducted on the vernal equinox to make sure the crops came in, or, according to other lore, worshipers of gods would erect totem figures of those gods at the edge of town, just so everyone knew who was running the show. Time went by, and those sacrifices or effigies turned into your friendly scarecrow dancing hand-in-hand with Dorothy down the Yellow Brick Road.

Well, maybe not in Burkittsville. Their scarecrow hopped right down off his pole and took his sacrifices with a sling blade. We nearly ended up on the wrong side of this Norse Billy Bob Thornton until we discovered that the Vanir was bound to a sacred tree— the first tree planted by Burkittsville's original settlers, back when they'd come over from Norway. Now, a tree we can handle; a little gas, a quick match, and the people of Burkittsville all of a sudden had to face the twenty-first century without their bloodthirsty guardian god.

Things are tough all over.

Lawrence

Home is where the heart is, right? Well, if you're from Lawrence, it's also where the spirits are. We've been lots of places, and pound for pound, Lawrence is one of the most haunted places on earth.

Hmm, where to begin . . .

How about Stull Cemetery?

America is full of haunted cemeteries. How could it not be? Cemeteries are full of dead people, and some of those people aren't ready to go. And we've nailed all kinds of ghosts and supernatural baddies in various graveyards. Certain cemeteries, though, seem to be—we'll just say they're more active than the norm. One is Bachelor's Grove in Chicago, home to ghosts as various as a woman in white and victims of Chicago's Prohibition-era gangsters. St. Louis Cemetery No. 1, in New Orleans, is home to another woman in white, who is also a vanishing hitchhiker. Old York Cemetery in York, Maine, is one of the few with an honest-to-god friendly ghost—apparently the spirit of a "wise woman" who died in 1774 but who still appears from time to time and gives children a push on the swing set next to the graveyard. McConnio Cemetery in Alabama hosts the ghosts of Civil War soldiers. A cemetery in Justice, Illinois, is home to Resurrection Mary, one of the most famous vanishing hitchhikers in the country.

There are more. Lots more. Stull Cemetery, though, has not only a haunted church but demonic apparitions and ghostly children to boot. The church has been abandoned since 1922 and without a roof for a long time; apparently, rain will not fall over it. And a crucifix that still hangs on the wall turns upside down at the approach of certain visitors. Creepy enough for you?

The Eldridge Hotel downtown stands on a cornerstone salvaged from the burned ruins of Lawrence after the infamous attack by Quantrill's Raiders in 1863, when the Confederate guerrillas attacked Lawrence and slaughtered around two hundred men and boys. It wasn't the worst thing that happened during the Civil War, but it was bad enough. Now the Eldridge is home to all kinds of spirits, especially on the fifth floor. We've heard stories of temperature changes, breath marks on the mirrors, and apparitions galore. If anyone harboring Confederate sympathies ever stays in room 506, we've got a feeling they're not going to get much sleep.

And then there's Haskell Indian Nations University, where every building is buzzing with the spirits of the Indian children who died there over the years. You can't take a step on that campus without your EMF reader going off the charts. The school, founded to strip Indian kids of their heritage and stir them into the American melting pot, was infamous for its cruelty. It has its own cemetery, where local shamans have tried for years to soothe the children's spirits, and it has other bodies as well. The University of Kansas has several skeletons of children in storage, dug up from Haskell's campus but absent from the university's attendance and death records. No one knows who they were, where they came from, or how they died, but you know what? We've got a feeling that one of these days, they're going to make themselves heard.

We'd never been to any of those places until a couple of years ago. Why? Because we hadn't been back to Lawrence since we left for New Mexico a couple of months after the Demon killed our mother. Dad never wanted to go back, and we were kids. We went where he went.

Until Sam had a dream.

It wasn't his first dream. That one was about Jessica. Specifically about her dying. But he kept it to himself. Tried to write it off. Then, a couple weeks later, the Demon got her. After that, he was ready to pay attention to the nightmare.

Sam dreamed of a woman trapped in a house, unable to get out. And in front of the house there was a tree. Something about the tree got to him, like he'd seen it before. Which he had: in a photograph of our old house in Lawrence.

The next day we were in Lawrence, and that's how we met Missouri Mosley, an old friend of Dad's. The first sentence of his journal, in fact, is, "I went to Missouri, and learned the truth." We'd always thought he meant he met someone in Missouri, but this someone who *was* Missouri turned out to be a psychic, and when we all got to the house, Missouri diagnosed the problem right away. There was not one, but *two* spirits in the house, attracted by the legacy of what happened to our mother.

It's like Missouri said: That kind of evil leaves a wound. And sometimes wounds get infected.

This infection was a poltergeist—and something else. What, we didn't know just yet.

You know about poltergeists. So do we. We've run into them here and there, and to tell you the truth, it's usually a pretty easy job. The last one we remember before coming home to Lawrence was in Pennsylvania, for a guy named Jerry. They're prankster ghosts, mostly. Throw things around, open and shut doors, spoil milk, that kind of thing. Theories about them range from psychokinesis—a child, usually, externalizing a trauma and creating a kind of thought-form—to a spirit of someone who died angry, so the ghost acts like it's having a tantrum all the time. The famous cases all seem to have something a little more serious about them, like the Demon Drummer of Tedworth, back in 1661, or the Borley Rectory in the 1820s.

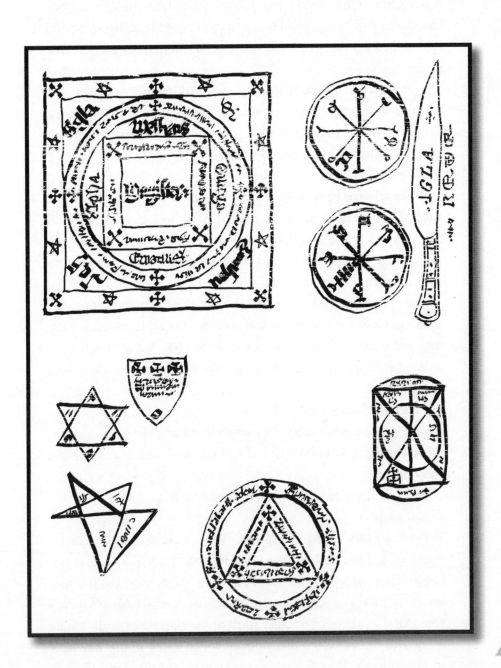

Poltergeists aren't always just jokers. Sometimes they're out for blood, like this one. It tried to trap a toddler in the refrigerator, and it munched a plumber's hand while he was fixing the garbage disposal.

And that was before Missouri got us working on getting rid of it. Because of the house's history, she said, it wasn't going to be enough to chase this one ghost. We were going to have to purify the house and make sure no other ghosts ever could get in.

Which is how we ended up sitting at her coffee table putting together gris-gris bags. Angelica root, good for removing curses and strengthening exorcisms, plus crossroads dirt to focus on the nexus between this world and the next—you get the drift. It might seem weird to be working up hoodoo charms against a poltergeist, but it's a weird business we're in.

The charms worked, sort of. The poltergeist seemed gone, but as things turned out, either it was stronger than the gris-gris or the bags just trapped it inside the house. Either way, we almost bought it. We were trapped in our old house. We got the family out, but we were stuck.

Then Mom saved us.

She was the other spirit. She stepped out and she gave us a moment to see her, to know that she still watched over us and that she was out there.

And then she annihilated herself to save us.

We've seen other vengeful spirits. We've wasted the spiritual remains of sadistic asylum directors, legendary serial killers, unreconstructed rednecks who never got over integration—the list goes on. Every time we hear of a strange series of deaths, odds are there's some kind of angry or unquiet spirit at the bottom of it all, *and it's always been that way*. Take this version, which dates all the way back to cuneiform tablets from Sumeria that record a being called an ekimmu. If you died violently, especially in a way that mutilated your body, you might find yourself turned into an ekimmu. Like the banshee, the ekimmu was a death omen, howling in the night as a sign that misfortune was on the way. Dad recorded a cuneiform inscription in his journal, listing various types of Sumerian spirits:

The wicked Utukku who slays man alive on the plain.
The wicked Alû who covers (man) like a garment.
The wicked Etimmu, the wicked Gallû, who bind the body.
The Lamme (Lamashtu), the Lammea (Labasu), who cause disease in the body.
The Lilû who wanders in the plain.
They have come nigh unto a suffering man on the outside.
They have brought about a painful malady in his body.
The curse of evil has come into his body.
An evil goblin they have placed in his body.
An evil bane has come into his body.
Evil poison they have placed in his body.
An evil malediction has come into his parts.
Evil and trouble they have placed in his body.
Poison and taint have come into his body.
They have produced evil.
Evil being, evil face, evil mouth, evil tongue.
Sorcery, venom, slaver, wicked machinations,
Which are produced in the body of the sick man.
O woe for the sick man whom they cause to moan like a šaharrat-pot.

Sometimes spirits turn evil if they died as children. We've run across a few of those, including the drowned boy in Lake Manitoc, Wisconsin, and more recently an angry little girl in a New England hotel. Years after she died, the owners of the hotel decided to shut it down, and boy, she made it clear she didn't want to go. Three or four dead bodies later, we showed up, and we found some things that you don't expect in white-picket-fence, small-town New England.

The first thing was a series of quincunxes in and around the hotel. A quincunx is an arrangement of dots—or anything, really—that looks like the five-spot on a die. Hoodoo practitioners use them to fix a spell in place by creating a symbolic crossroads to enhance the magical potential of a particular location. That's what was going on in that hotel, and the little girl spirit was indulging in some image magic, too, using her playmate's collection of dolls to bring hotel guests—not to mention representatives of the people who wanted to buy the place—to gruesome and untimely ends.

The Mordechai Murdock tulpa.

Dean takes care of a zombie using the silver stake method.

A vengeful spirit who possessed a family portrait.

Bloody Mary.

A Vanir.

A shapeshifter, playing dead.

A shapeshifter gets ready to change out of its 'Dean' form.

A vengeful/homicidal spirit.

A wendigo.

The Hook Man.

The second thing we found was an old woman, squirreled away like the crazy aunt in *Wuthering Heights* (who said we never read a book?) and wearing a hoodoo necklace. That's when we started to put things together and realized that the owner's daughter wasn't kidding when she talked about having an imaginary friend. Turned out that this girl had died in the hotel and couldn't stand the idea of her playmate—now the old hoodoo-wearing woman—leaving her behind. So she started killing everybody in sight.

Kids, man. They're tough. Eventually, we realized that like the drowned boy in Wisconsin, this one wouldn't just go away without a sacrifice. All we could do was watch as the old lady went to join her friend. It wasn't one of our more satisfying jobs.

By and large, child spirits are among the baddest of the bad, maybe because there's so much potential in their souls that when it curdles, it really curdles. Here's another kind of child spirit that we ran across in Dad's journal while figuring this one out.

MYLING. Scandinavian child spirit, also called UTBURD. Typically the souls of murdered children, or children who died unbaptized. They will ride with travelers at night and demand to be taken to a graveyard so they can rest, but they get heavier and heavier as the graveyard gets closer, until the person carrying them is driven under the earth by their weight. This belief is derived from the practice of leaving unwanted or deformed infants out to die of exposure. Generally they haunt the location where they were abandoned, but folklore also notes their presence in the dwellings of those who killed them—usually a family member. If their remains can be located and buried in hallowed ground, they will disappear.

Death Apparitions

Not all spirits are out for revenge. Sometimes they just want justice. Take the case of a woman named Claire Becker, murdered by her lover, who was a crooked cop in Baltimore. We had to do a little more interacting with the local PD than is usually our preference, mostly because they thought we were serial killers.

Until one of the Baltimore cops, Diana Ballard, saw the ghost of Claire Becker. That bought us enough slack so that we could do some investigating and discover that Claire's murderer was Ballard's partner.

Awkward.

The way it all came together was that we figured out that Claire wasn't a vengeful spirit—she'd had plenty of chances to off all of us by then. She was a death omen, a spirit that appears to people to warn them of their doom—which in this case meant warn everyone involved that Ballard's partner, Peter Sheridan, was gunning for them.

Some death omens are quiet. They don't all howl like your proverbial banshee. An apparition of an individual can signal that person's death. The Germanic doppelgänger, the Scandinavian *vardogr*, the Icelandic *fylgja*, the Finnish *etiäinen*, they're all manifestations of bilocation: the phenomenon of appearing in two places at once. Sometimes bilocation is the result of distress; the *etiäinen* generally appears when a shaman or someone in extreme circumstances is reaching out to the person with whom they share the closest emotional relationship. It's not a big step from there to a death omen. Most apparitions of doubles foreshadow death in one way or another. Sometimes the apparition appears suffering the wounds that the person will die of, but more often the plain fact of the apparition is enough to signal that death is near.

Sometimes a death apparition appears to warn other people, like in Claire Becker's case. We got the message just in time, as it turned out, and Diana settled things with Officer Sheridan before she could meet an untimely death.

In other cases, spirits are summoned, usually accidentally, often by people they loved, and the spirits just do what they think people want them to do. The problem is that they pick up on all the wrong signals, and one thing about spirits is that they kind of lose track of whatever moral compass they might have had in real life. We worked a real strange case not too long ago in which the spirit was a pastor who was causing problems (read: killing people) because in the spirit world it was no longer able to distinguish right from wrong. Spirits just understand desire.

So what we had to do was talk to it. In other words, perform a séance.

Now when we say séance, we don't mean the circle around a table where some John Edward type fishes around for clues about what his audience might want to hear. There are real rituals for contacting the dead in most religious traditions, and we've learned a few of them. The one we used to contact the dead pastor came from a primitive Christian rite. We found this version of it in Dad's journal:

> On a clean altar cloth inscribed with the symbols as above, place a small bowl filled with fresh herbs. Around the perimeter of the cloth, place black and white candles, alternating and equal in number. When all of the candles are lit, recite the following:
>
> AMATE SPIRITUS OBSCURE, TE QUAERIMUS.
> TE ORAMUS, NOBISCUM COLLOQUERE, APUD
> NOS CIRCITA.
>
> At the finish of the incantation, pinch a tiny amount of frankincense, sandalwood, or cinnamon powder over one of the candle flames.

We chose that one because we were working in a Christian framework that time. You want voodoo? We've got voodoo, too. Winchester and Sons is a full-service outfit.

MONSTERS

If something isn't undead, and it isn't really a spirit, and it isn't really a demon, what is it? The best word we can come up with is "monster." Now, this is a fluid category, we'll grant you that. But to us, a spirit is something that died and refuses to leave. A demon is something that lives in hell and only comes topside to spread pain and chaos. And a revenant is something dead that won't lie down.

The other kind of sucker's a monster.

The word "monster" comes from the Latin *monstrum*, which means—well, it means "monster," but it also means "portent" or "omen." Bad sign. From a root, *monere*, that means "warn." People used to think that monsters were signs of impending disaster. Our experience has been a little different. We think that monsters are disasters all by themselves. Nothing impending about them.

The world is full of monsters, and also full of people pretending there are monsters where there aren't any. That's part of the fun. Are there lake monsters? You bet there are. We've seen them. We've never been to Scotland, so we can't tell you if Nessie is for real, and the same goes for Argentina and Nahuelito, but as far as Champ goes—you ever hear of Champ? Head up to Lake Champlain sometime and ask around. You'll get an earful. Back in 1609 or so, Samuel de Champlain saw the monster while exploring the lake that would later bear his name. Since then, Indian legends and tourist reports have consistently said that something's in the lake.

Giants and ogres? Never seen one.

Dragons? Give us a break.

But cryptozoologists would probably say the same thing about, say, an evil spirit. So who are we to say? There are more things in heaven and earth, et cetera, et cetera. Or, to put it another way, here's what astronomer Arthur Eddington said about the general bizarritude of everything: "The universe is not only stranger than we imagine, it is stranger than we *can* imagine."

Wendigo

Wendigo stories break down into two categories. In one, the wendigo is created when a proud warrior trades his soul for the power to destroy a threat to his tribe. Once the threat is gone, he is driven into the wilderness and vanishes. In the other, the wendigo slowly loses its humanity through some combination of dark magic and cannibalism. In either case, the end result is one fearsome monster.

Cryptozoologists have seized on the wendigo legends as evidence for everything from Sasquatch to the survival of D. B. Cooper, and although they're wrong—don't get us started on cryptozoologists—there is some variation in the appearance of individual wendigo. They don't look like Bigfoot. More like a yeti, maybe, that's eaten nothing but snow since 1850. They're typically larger than a human, but not too much, and skeletally thin. Often, especially in the north country, they are missing some of the body parts that are most vulnerable to frostbite: toes and parts of the ears and nose. Sometimes they're covered in matted white fur, and other descriptions characterize them as practically hairless. What all of the descriptions have in common is inhumanly long teeth, claws instead of fingernails, and glowing eyes.

Often they hunt by simply running down their prey, but sometimes there's a different approach, one that for our money says that the *wendigo* enjoys what it does. A lone traveler in the forest starts to hear things, say. He looks around and never quite sees anything, except every once in a while he catches a glimpse of something moving fast out of the corner of his eye. After a while all of these glimpses add up, and maybe the *wendigo* gives him a growl to get things going a little faster. The traveler snaps at last and begins to run, and then the *wendigo* pounces.

They don't have to do it that way. *Wendigo* are stronger and faster than any human alive and can kill you before you know they're in the same time zone. They do it that way because they like to.

And if you survive an encounter with a *wendigo*, don't think you're out of the woods yet (ha). There's plenty of lore claiming that the *wendigo* can possess the spirits of hunters, jumping bodies, perhaps, when its own has started to break down.

So how do you kill them? Part of the final transformation from human to *wendigo* is the heart changing into pure ice. Shatter that icy heart with a blade of iron or silver, and you kill the *wendigo*.

Maybe. The only way to be sure is to cut its body apart. Us Winchesters, we're of the opinion that it never hurts to burn them, too.

After his first run-in with a *wendigo*, Dad had this to say:

Algernon Blackwood wrote a famous horror story called "The Wendigo." We got a kick out of it but have to agree with Dad, too—once you've really seen a *wendigo,* some of the zip is gone from the story.

We've taken out a *wendigo,* and it wasn't easy. Hunters who don't bat an eyelash at your average spirit speak of the *wendigo* with the kind of respect due a dangerous adversary. And speaking of hunters, one of the legends from the job was Jack Fiddler, a Cree Indian who claimed at least fourteen *wendigo* kills—the last in 1907, when he was eighty-seven years old. That one got him thrown in prison, which we can tell you is still one of the perpetual hazards of the family business.

Another winter spirit is the *yuki-onna.* It's from Japan. Typically appearing as a beautiful woman, the *yuki-onna* is possibly the spirit of someone who has died of exposure—although we're not quite sure why they're always female. Don't men ever freeze to death in Japan? Her modus operandi: she appears to people who have gotten lost in a snowstorm and either kills them outright or leads them on, promising shelter, until they die. A variation on the lore says that she appears to a parent searching for a lost child, and in this manifestation she holds a child in her arms. When the grateful parent takes the child from her, he or she is frozen in place and dies.

Occasionally her predations take on a sexual flavor, and she leads men to what seems to be a shelter and then, well, you know. Kills them. But not right away.

A slightly more merciful incarnation of the *yuki-onna* tells of a young boy lost in a storm. The spirit finds the boy and lets him go because of his youth, on the condition that he never tell anyone that he has seen her. He agrees, but years later, he tells his wife the story—whereupon his wife turns out to be the *yuki-onna*. Again she spares him because he is a good father to the children they have reared together, but because he has broken his promise, she disappears, melting away as if she were made of ice.

Shapeshifters

Where do we start with the shapeshifters? We've tangled with them twice—three times if you count the *rakshasa*—and none of 'em were exactly a day at the park. Especially the part where we had an entire SWAT team on our ass while we were hunting the thing in a bank full of panicked hostages.

The skinwalker is the type we're most familiar with. It doesn't change into a wolf or a monster or anything else nonhuman. What it does is kill people and assume their shapes. When it does this, it has to shed its current skin. Skinwalkers die just like people, but the problem is, you never know for sure that you're capping off the right person. That kind of uncertainty wears on you after a while.

The one way we know to recognize them is that their eyes give off a strange luminescence when they're viewed on security cameras or other video devices. We don't think they know this, but you can never be too careful.

What sets skinwalkers apart is just how boring they are when you get right down to it. If you could change shape, would you use that ability to get rich? That's what the one in the bank did. Not exactly the most original idea, considering the crazy (and way more fun) options open to you if you can switch faces with anyone you want. Anyway, we ran across this little gem from Dad's journal, which kind of says it all.

And usually those transformations are into other forms, but there are some varieties of this critter that can raise hell in human form, too.

▶ YENALDOOSHI

First and foremost among those is the *yenaldooshi*, native to the Navajo regions of the Southwest.

Like some *wendigo* and the loup-garou, the *yenaldooshi* gains su-pernatural power by violating a serious cultural taboo, in this case murdering a relative. The *yenaldooshi* are shamans and nec-romancers who spread sickness by means of a powder made from corpses. For the Navajo, who revere pollen, this is a deep sacrilege. The *yenaldooshi* can also make tiny pellets out of bone. Get one of those under your skin, and you've got problems ahead. Most *yenaldooshi* can turn into coyotes, and some of them have other shape-changing abil-ities as well.

▶ BEARWALKER

In northern Michigan, Chippewa legend tells of bearwalkers, usually shamans of some kind who gain the power of shapeshifting—almost always into a bear, but occasionally into an owl as well. You can spot a bearwalker because when they're on the way to work their magic, they breathe spectral fire. Anyone who gets too close to the bearwalker will be paralyzed and fall to the ground, unless they have medicine to counteract it. And if you do, and can get your arms around the bearwalker, it will revert to human form.

> The bearwalker visits four times, four days apart. Around the victim's house, family members will see a light moving in the trees. After the fourth visit, the victim dies. Four days after the victim is buried, the bearwalker must visit the grave and recover part of the body—usually one finger and the tip of the tongue—or he too will die, after four months have passed.

This is another way of identifying and eliminating them, but it's not one we like. Our job is to save people, and it's definitely not cool to wait until you've already lost a loved one before joining the hunt.

Bearwalkers are vulnerable to being shot, but it takes a tough *hombre* to withstand the bearwalker's magic long enough to aim a gun. More often than not, you fall over and lie on the side of the road while the bearwalker strolls past you on its way to finish its charm. If you do manage to shoot it, it will disappear, heading off somewhere lonely to die. Sometimes that's how the local Indians know who was a bearwalker, when word spreads that one was shot and a sudden disappearance follows.

On a lighter note, sometimes the bearwalker uses its powers to win over a reluctant lover. Here's a story Dad overheard while he was traveling in Michigan's Upper Peninsula:

> Outside L'Anse, in a roadhouse full of Indians from the lumber camp down the way:
>
> There was a white woman named Jennie who had an Indian working for her—a shiftless, lazy Sioux. She hated him so much that if he was at the table, she wouldn't sit down, but he bragged down around the docks that he was going to have her. All I have to do, he said, is go into the woods and find the right root, and you'll see. I'll have that Jennie. Well, all of his buddies down at the docks, they made fun of him, but pretty soon he started leaving little candies around the table, and Jennie would eat them when he wasn't around so he wouldn't know she was doing it, and wouldn't you know it, all of a sudden—wasn't but a couple of months later—she up and married him. Then, when he had her in his power, he treated her real bad, almost starved her to death. He worked his bearwalk on one of her relatives, too, and that was enough. They took care of him, and we didn't ever see him around here no more.

Well, maybe that note isn't so much lighter after all. Sounds to us like the Indians in Michigan have their own hunters. We'll have to drop by sometime, compare notes. Maybe see if there're still any bearwalkers around.

▶ *LESZY*

The *leszy* is a Slavic forest spirit that can appear as any animal or plant. One of his preferred shapes is a talking mushroom, which is funny until you know that the *leszy* is more than capable of killing people whom it considers to be abusing its woodlands. Sometimes it settles for playing pranks, such as making people nauseous or hiding lumberjacks' axes, but when it's in a lethal mood, the *leszy* has been known to tickle people to death. Not a way we'd want to go—not that we particularly want to go at all. Still, *tickling!?*

Some of the *leszy*'s other common shapes are a tall tree or a human with a beard of vines. Occasionally he sports hooves and horns. He can command wolves and bears. When in regular human form, his only telltale signs are glowing eyes and—if you can look away from his eyes—shoes worn backward.

Unlike some fairy shapechangers, the *leszy* has a family: *leszachka*, his wife, and *leshonky*, his children. All are dangerous if they feel that they or the forest is threatened. And, if you can get on their good side, they will protect your animals and crops. They might even teach you some magic.

▶ NAHUALES

Aztec and other pre-conquest Mexican mythologies are chock-full of shapeshifters, each with a different totem animal depending on the *nahual*'s birthday. In the Aztec calendar, various days are named after animals, and we've heard of *nahuales* who could take the forms of eagles, jaguars, snakes, coyotes, you name it. If it lives in Mexico, there's probably a person somewhere who can change into it.

In Aztec myth, the *nahuales* were the protectors and servants of Tezcatlipoca, one of the foremost gods of war and sacrifice. (The god's name means something like "smoke mirror" and refers to an Aztec method of divination using bowls of mercury.) The *nahuales* were hunted during and after the conquest, when a special arm of the Inquisition was set up to eliminate them. Not only are they shapeshifters, but more often than not, they're sorcerers and necromancers as well. One of

the most famous was Nezahualcoyotl, "The Fasting Coyote," who was a philosopher-king of Texcoco and who—after his official "death" in 1472—was still said to be advising Montezuma at the time of the conquest. According to the same stories, Nezahualcoyotl survived the conquest and disappeared to fight again another day.

Nahuales aren't like werewolves in that they don't infect people with their bite. They're more likely just to kill you. And then, when you're dead, they might call up your spirit and put it to work for them. Nasty critters.

▶ PUCA

The *puca* has some features in common with the *each uisge* and kelpie, in that it tries to get travelers onto its back and then takes them for terrifying rides. We've never been able to figure out these stories. If you were walking alone in the woods late at night, and a weird critter appeared and wanted you to get on its back so it could take you for a ride, would *you* do it? We didn't think so. But apparently, not everyone feels the same way, because people are always getting taken for the rides of their lives. Unlike the water spirits, the *puca* doesn't automatically kill its riders—but that isn't out of the question. It can appear as an eagle or a goat, but is usually seen as a black horse with glowing yellow eyes.

We're *very* interested in stories about supernatural beings with glowing yellow eyes. Dad was too:

> Puca seems to be a distant cousin of the wild hunt.
> Quebec version, CHASSE-GALERIE, where an unlucky lumberjack gets taken for a ride with the devil on a haunted canoe. Wild hunt riders recruit accidental viewers to join them, and some can never leave. Often there's a warning not to leave until a certain event has occurred,

The *puca* can speak, and if offended, it will come to the home of the offender and demand that the offender come for a ride. If refused, it will destroy crops and ruin the homestead. It also demands certain annual sacrifices. If crops are brought in after Samhain (which you post-pagans know as Halloween, but which originally was a celebration of bringing in the last harvest), the *puca* will be angry, and it is traditional to consider anything remaining in the fields on November 1 property of the *puca*. Some farmers also leave part of their crops unharvested as an offering. If these protocols are followed, the *puca* may appear on November 1 and offer prophecies.

▶ THE ANIMAL WIFE: *SELKIES,* SWAN MAIDENS, *KITSUNE*

"Swan maiden" is kind of a generic term for all kinds of shapeshifting creatures who are sometimes animals and sometimes gorgeous women. In Italy, it's a dove, in Croatia a wolf, in parts of Africa a buffalo. The stories have in common the theft of the skin (or robe of feathers), the swan maiden having to marry and bear children for whoever possesses the skin, the rediscovery of the skin when the children are a little older, and the swan maiden's abandoning of the children. Sometimes her husband goes after her and after great hardship brings her back. Sometimes she's just gone for good.

Anywhere there are seals, there are *selkie* stories, and they all follow a basic pattern. The *selkie*, if it's female, transforms into a human to take a human lover. She must protect her sealskin, however, because without it she can't change back. If the human lover discovers the skin and is able to hide it from the *selkie*, she is now in his power. However much she loves the man, a *selkie* always loves the sea more and will immediately return to it if she discovers her skin. In many of the stories, the *selkie* bears children, and it is one of the children who discovers the skin. Typically *selkies* will not speak to their former lovers once they return to the sea, although they can meet and maintain contact with the children.

All very tragic, right? Well, let us tell you a story. We were in Maine one summer, and stories started to get around about two fishermen who had been attacked and killed—by seals. Our dad being who he was, he started sniffing around, and since we were bored with collecting seashells and playing Skee-Ball, we did, too. Turns out that not only had a local man taken a *selkie* wife, but he'd passed her down through his family. She'd been on land for more than a hundred years, always looking out at the ocean and yearning to return home.

And during that hundred years, seventeen other men from that family had disappeared at sea. The people in the town talked about curses, but they didn't know the half of it. We figured it out when we saw pictures of the *selkie* from 1903, then 1929, then 1960, and then 1993. All the same beautiful face, in three different towns with three different husbands. Things came to a head when her current husband decided he was going to go out with some friends and shoot some seals. We showed up at the same time, having found the sealskin just beforehand, and brokered a deal. The *selkie* got to go home, and the rest of her people agreed to stop their war on the men of the family.

We don't know how it's all going to turn out, though, because that kind of bad blood runs deep, and also because another thing *selkies* occasionally do is slip changeling children into the cribs of seaside villages. They keep the human child who knows where, and when the *selkie* child gets to be a certain age, *poof!* It changes into a seal and is never seen again.

And then there's the *kitsune*, a Japanese fox spirit who can act as a lover, a trickster, or a succubus, depending on the story. *Kitsune* can take human form, except often they have trouble hiding their tails, which can complicate the kind of deception necessary to capture a human. (Well, most humans.) Sometimes *kitsune* feed off the life force of the men they seduce, and sometimes they marry and settle down. The *kitsune* can be a devoted wife, but the marriages are always doomed because sooner or later—you guessed it—hubby notices the tail. Then the *kitsune* has to leave, or in other versions the man suddenly awakens from the *kitsune*'s enchantment, far from home and destined for a very interesting conversation with the human family he left behind.

A *kitsune*'s magical abilities and (blame Dean for this; he can't help it) foxy temperament mean that they're fierce tricksters. Some of their favorite targets are pompous men, the greedy and boastful types. This playfulness can turn dark, though, and *kitsune* are also known to play cruel tricks on people who don't deserve it at all. The more powerful of them have truly marvelous magical abilities, including the ability to bend time and space (as in the case of the poor tail-discovering ex-husband we just mentioned).

So how do you control a spirit that can change shape, appear in dreams, and wrap reality around its little finger? Well, some *kitsune* are constantly guarding a *hoshi no tama*, or "star ball." Like a *selkie*'s skin, if you've got a *kitsune*'s star ball, you can make it do whatever you want. Thing is, we're not sure what the star ball really is, or what it's supposed to do. If we ever run into a *kitsune*, we'll let you know.

▶ LYCANTHROPY

Any country or region that has wolves seems also to have werewolves. Also werebears, wereowls, were-*whatevers*. The amount of folklore is so overwhelming and contradictory that it's hard to figure out what to do about them—except through plain old trial and error.

Medieval werewolf legends usually equate lycanthropy with sorcery, and with the wearing of a magical skin or belt. Dad made a note about Richard Verstegan's *Restitution of Decayed Intelligence*, from 1628:

Verstegan says werewolves "are certayne sorcerers, who having annoynted their bodies with an ointment which they make by the instinct of the devil, and putting on a certayne inchaunted girdle, does not only unto the view of others seem as wolves, but to their own thinking have both the shape and nature of wolves, so long as they wear the said girdle. And they do dispose themselves as very wolves, in worrying and killing, and most of humane creatures." Verstegan hints that the werewolf has no conscious memory of its actions while it is transformed— "to their own thinking." Other accounts, not Verstegan's, have this hand-in-hand with a belief that werewolves can only transform while they are asleep.

Later, the belief in a werewolf belt faded and was replaced with the idea that werewolves turn on their own, often on a full moon. This wasn't a new invention, though. The Roman writer Petronius, in his *Satyricon*, mentions the following story of a man

who turns into a wolf at the full moon—so the idea's been around at least since then.

My master had gone to Capua to sell some old clothes. I seized the opportunity, and persuaded our guest to bear me company about five miles out of town; for he was a soldier, and as bold as death. We set out about cockcrow, and the moon shone bright as day, when, coming among some monuments, my man began to converse with the stars, whilst I jogged along singing and counting them. Presently I looked back after him, and saw him strip and lay his clothes by the side of the road. My heart was in my mouth in an instant, I stood like a corpse; when, in a crack, he was turned into a wolf. Don't think I'm joking: I would not tell you a lie for the finest fortune in the world.

But to continue: after he was turned into a wolf, he set up a howl and made straight for the woods. At first I did not know whether I was on my head or my heels; but at last going to take up his clothes, I found them turned into stone. The sweat streamed from me, and I never expected to get over it. Melissa began to wonder why I walked so late. "Had you come a little sooner," she said, "you might at least have lent us a hand; for a wolf broke into the farm and has butchered all our cattle; but though he got off, it was no laughing matter for him, for a servant of ours ran him through with a pike." Hearing this I could not close an eye; but as soon as it was daylight, I ran home like a pedlar that has been eased of his pack. Coming to the place where the clothes had been turned into stone, I saw nothing but a pool of blood; and when I got home, I found my soldier lying in bed, like an ox in a stall, and a surgeon dressing his neck. I saw at once that he was a fellow who could change his skin, and never after could I eat bread with him, no, not if you would have killed me. Those who would have taken a different view of the case are welcome to their opinion; if I tell you a lie, may your genii confound me!

Like Verstegan, Russian stories tend to paint the werewolf transformation as voluntary and sorcerous. Here's an interesting little spell, if you ever want to try it:

He who desires to become an OBOROT, let him seek in the forest a hewn-down tree; let him stab it with a small copper knife, and walk round the tree, repeating the following incantation:

On the sea, on the ocean, on the island, on Buyan,
On the empty pasture gleams the moon, on an
   ashstock lying
In a green wood, in a gloomy vale.
Towards the stock wandereth a shaggy wolf,
Horned cattle seeking for his sharp white fangs;
But the wolf enters not the forest,
But the wolf dives not into the shadowy vale,
Moon, moon, gold-horned moon,
Check the flight of bullets, blunt the hunters'
   knives,
Break the shepherds' cudgels,
Cast wild fear upon all cattle,
On men, all creeping things,
That they may not catch the grey wolf,
That they may not rend his warm skin!
My word is binding, more binding than sleep,
More binding than the promise of a hero!

Then he springs thrice over the tree and runs into the forest, transformed into a wolf.

In the New World, werewolf legends tend to center on isolation from and rejection by humans, often with insinuations that people who become werewolves have been up to unsavory things. This doesn't happen just in the Americas, either; Armenian folklore tells of women who, as a consequence of some deadly sin, suffer visitations from spirits that force them to transform into wolves and kill children. A New World example of this is the French-Canadian legend of the loup-garou, which has variations all over North America, a creature said to be created when someone refused the sacraments for a certain period of time. The loup-garou comes from France—duh—which has one of the most active werewolf traditions in Europe. French court records are full of werewolf trials, and that's not even counting the Beast of Gévaudan, which killed as many as eighty people in the 1760s.

Loup-garou legends from precolonial Illinois say that after the initial transformation, a loup-garou was doomed to 101 nights of transformation, followed by days of melancholia and sickness. The only way to get out of the sentence early was if someone managed to draw blood from the loup-garou, and in this case, neither party involved could ever speak of the incident until the remainder of the 101 days had passed. There's even a Cajun version called a rougarou, which lives in the bayous and can transform into a kind of were-crocodile. Like the loup-garou, the rouga-rou is often a man transformed because of a rejection by human society, especially religious beliefs.

> Werewolves will avoid wolfsbane when they can, as well as holy artifacts and silver. Being stabbed or cut with a silver knife can sometimes force a werewolf to revert to human shape. The silver bullet legend is probably true, but not all hunters believe in it. You hear grumbles around the gathering places. I was at Harvelle's not too long ago and heard three hunters complaining that either they'd done something wrong when they made their silver bullets, or some werewolves just weren't affected.
>
> Lycanthropy might have a cure. According to some traditions, killing a particular werewolf removes its curse on all those it's bitten—severing the bloodline, in a way.

The one time we put that theory to the test, it didn't work. The werewolf in question was a receptionist named Madison Owens. Nice girl, went walking in the wrong part of town on a full-moon night, got mugged. What she didn't know was that her attacker was a werewolf, and he managed to take a bite out of her neck. Next lunar cycle, she started turning. Worst part was, she had no idea. She turned after she fell asleep, and woke with no memory of roaming the streets in were form, ripping the heart out of anyone who registered as a threat to her animal instinct.

We did our best. Dean hunted down the werewolf who'd bitten Madison. Shot him through the heart with a silver bullet. But it didn't work. And by then, a lot had gone on between Sam and Madison. They'd connected. He was ready to do whatever it took to save her. Unfortunately, there was nothing. At least as far as we could find. We scoured every source, called every hunter we knew. Seems like if you're a werewolf, there's no cure.

That severing-the-bloodline legend sure is sticky, though. It comes up again and again. We think it originates from the old European idea that if you kill the daddy vampire of a particular infestation, the rest of the nest will die (well, re-die) too.

Of course, then we'd just have to start in on all the rest of the world's dangerous shapechangers. *Hamrammr, boudas, aswang, bruxsa, ilimu, kanima*—you're next.

Tulpas and Other Created Beings

They say that if enough people believe something, it's true. Well, politicians say that. Those of us who try to work with real things in the real world aren't as convinced, but we have to admit that it's possible to create something just by believing in it hard enough. In the Tibetan mystical tradition, highly advanced lamas and naturally gifted laymen could give their thoughts and imaginings an actual physical existence. They're called *tulpas*, and they're tricky to handle.

A *tulpa* is, pure and simple, a being created by the act of someone imagining it. When the two of us were kids, we never had imaginary friends because the real world was just too damn weird, and we didn't want to make it any weirder. But—understatement alert—most kids aren't like we were, and every once in a while, the kind of process that creates an imaginary friend goes a little farther.

It's not just Tibetans who believe this, either. We found these two quotes side-by-side in Dad's journal and were never sure what they meant until we ran into the *tulpa*:

> Determined will is the beginning of all magical operations. . . . It is because men do not perfectly imagine and believe the result, that

> *the arts [of magic] are uncertain, while they*
> *might be perfectly certain.*
> —Paracelsus

> All things are possible to him that believeth.
> —Mark 9:23

Later, Dad runs through some thoughts about *tulpas*. Thought-forms are central to many magical practices. One in particular, eidolonic necromancy, is almost all about creating thoughtforms through magically intensified visualizations of certain spirits. Helena Blavatsky and other Theosophists—who were a bunch of wackos, by the way, but they stumbled across some truth because, as Bobby Singer said to us one day, even a blind pig gets an acorn once in a while—believed that they had created thoughtforms of all kinds of different astral beings. The Crowley school of occult practice is full of instances of created beings, too. About the *tulpa* specifically, Dad notes:

> TULPA created through intense ritual visualizations known as DUBTHAB. Variation known as DRAGPOI DUBTHAB is specifically aimed at creating a thought-form with the idea of harming another person. Physical form of TULPA becomes apparent to the senses after the mind can begin to sense its spirit presence. TULPA thus created, no matter the creator's intent, will gradually turn on the creator.

We've gone back and forth over the question of whether poltergeists are a kind of *tulpa*. We're still not sure. Poltergeists are often created when traumatized kids externalize their trauma; seems to us that you've got a thoughtform there. But sometimes other spirits act like poltergeists, so it's hard to nail down the differences. What we do know is that a *tulpa* isn't anchored to anything the way a spirit is. There's no bones to burn or haunted objects to destroy.

In the case of the particular *tulpa* we dealt with, a guy named Mordechai Murdock, we found out that he was created, in a way, by the Internet. Some yahoos in Richardson, Texas, faked up a haunted house/murdering spirit story, and then some I-want-to-believe types had bought the story and put it up on a Web site. Enough people believed it that—*presto!*—the fictional killer became real. Once we knew that, we went back and looked at some of the loony graffiti painted all over the house and found a Tibetan spirit sigil used in mystical traditions to focus thought and belief. That's how we got our *tulpa*, we thought, and decided that maybe if we destroyed the sigil, we'd get the *tulpa*.

No such luck. Once created, *tulpas* have a life of their own. But what we figured out was that since the *tulpa* is a product of intense and focused belief, if you change what its creator (in this case creators) believe, then you change the *tulpa*. So we put out a nerd-grapevine memo that old Mordechai had shot himself and was still so scared of guns that a consecrated iron bullet would kill him. That almost worked—the bullets slowed him down for a minute, anyway—but the server crashed and so did everyone's belief in that particular bit of the Mordechai story.

So what did we do? We went back to basics. Burned the goddamn place down around his ears.

Once a *tulpa* achieves physical form it starts acting like a rebellious teenager. More often than not, it wants to get out from under the control of its creator, and you can guess where that goes. In this case, its creators were distributed all over the world, so that wasn't a problem, but take the lesson to heart. If you're sitting at home right now thinking really hard about creating a *tulpa* with those certain qualities you find missing in your current friends and loved ones, remember: Life isn't like *Weird Science*. It's more like *Frankenstein*.

Homunculus

From Tibetan mysticism into European alchemy—who says we never got any education? The first use of the word "homunculus" occurs in the writings of the alchemist Paracelsus, who claimed that he had manufactured a foot-high humanoid, akin to a golem but not as big. After a few days, the homunculus attacked him and ran away, never to be seen again.

This is one of the problems with homunculi: they don't stick around. Sometimes, if you force them to by imprisoning them, they just up and die. Other homunculus creations live out their entire lives in jars and die if they are removed, as in this weirdo little story taken from Dad's journal:

Got this one from one Emil Besetzny, who published a book in 1873 about homunculi created by John Ferdinand, count of Kueffstein [if there wasn't a place called Kueffstein, someone would have to make it up], in about 1775. Besetzny's sources were apparently Masonic manuscripts and the journal of the count's butler, who went by the name of Kammerer. The count's collaborating alchemist was a Rosicrucian monk by the name of Abbe Geloni:

The bottles were closed with ox-bladders, and with a great magic seal [Solomon's seal?]. The spirits swam about in those bottles, and were about one span long. . . . They were therefore buried under two cartloads of horse manure, and the pile daily sprinkled with a certain liquor, prepared with great trouble by the two adepts, and made out of some "very disgusting materials.". . . After the bottles were removed, the "spirits" had grown to be each one about one and a half span long, so that the bottles were almost too small to contain them, and the male homunculi had come into possession of heavy beards, and the nails of their fingers and toes had grown a great deal. . . . In the bottle of the red and in that of the blue spirit, however, there was nothing to be seen but "clear water"; but whenever the Abbe knocked three times at the seal upon the mouth of the bottles, speaking at the same time some Hebrew words, the water in the bottle began to turn blue (respectively red), and the blue and the red spirits would show their faces, first very small, but growing in proportions until they attained the size of an ordinary human face. The face of the blue sprite was beautiful, like an angel, but the face of the red one bore a horrible expression.

Once every week the water had to be removed, and the bottles filled again with pure rainwater. This change had to be accomplished very rapidly, because during the few moments that the spirits were exposed to the air they closed their eyes, and seemed to become weak and unconscious, as if they were about to die. But the blue spirit was never fed, nor was the water changed; while the red one received once a week a thimbleful of fresh blood of some animal (chicken), and this blood disappeared in the water as soon as it was poured into it. . . .

The spirits gave prophecies about future events that usually proved to be correct. They knew the most secret things, but each of them was only acquainted with such things as belonged to his station; for instance, the king could talk politics, the monk about religion, the miner about minerals & etc.; but the red and blue spirits seemed to know about everything.

By some accident the glass containing the monk fell one day upon the floor and was broken. The poor monk died after a few painful respirations, in spite of all the efforts of the count to save his life, and his body was buried in the garden. An attempt to generate another one, made by the count without the assistance of the Abbe, who had left, resulted in a failure, as it produced only a small thing like a leech, which had very little vitality and soon died.

Interested in making a homunculus? Several recipes have come down through the ages. Paracelsus had the simplest one. Take a bag of bones, sperm, skin fragments, and hair of any animal that you want the homunculus to look like. Bury it, cover in horse manure, remove at forty days. You'll have an embryonic homunculus. Then you just have to feed it, usually by keeping a ready supply of more horse manure around. Yeah, sounds appetizing.

Other recipes involve the addition of mandrake root—a powerful intensifier of magic, and popularly believed to grow on ground used for hangings. The root must be picked before dawn by a black dog (there's that black dog again) and steeped in milk, honey, and blood. This will develop it into a homunculus that will protect the creator. Other versions incubated homunculi in chicken eggs in which part of the egg white was replaced with one or more of the ingredients from the other recipes.

Bottom line? We don't recommend you make a homunculus.

Golem

We don't think we'll ever see a golem, because you have to be holy as all get-out to create one, and we don't run into too many holy people. Since we're talking about homunculi, though, the golem lore is worth a mention, too.

There isn't any identifiable "first" golem story. Adam was created from dust and kneaded into the shape of a man, according to the Talmud, so from one perspective all humans are golems, or descended from golems. But as time went on, only the wisest and purest of rabbis would attempt the creation of a golem.

Dad made some notes about golems while he was looking into homunculi and alchemy:

> Most golems can't speak. Idea is that if granted speech, they would have a soul, and that an imperfect creation (created by man rather than God) would have an imperfect soul and be dangerous.
>
> From Sanhedrin 65b:
>
> Rava stated: If they wish, Tzadikkim could create a world. Rava created a man and he sent it to Rabi Zeira. Rabi Zeira spoke with it and it did not respond. Rabi Zeira then stated, "You are

created by my colleague, return to your dust." Rav Chanina and Rav Oshiah would sit every Friday and study the Sefer Yetzirah and create a calf that has reached a third of its potential development and subsequently eat it.

Eleazar of Worms mentions golems in commentary on Sefer Yetzirah:

Whoever studies Sefer Yetzirah has to purify himself, don white robes. It is forbidden to study alone, but only in two's and three's, as it is written, . . . and the beings they made in Haran, (Genesis 12:5), and as it is written, two are better than one (Ecclesiastes 4:9), and as it is written, it is not good for man to be alone; I will make a fitting helper for him (Genesis 2:18). For this reason Scripture begins with a "bet"—"Bereshit bara," He created.

It is required that he take virgin soil from a place in the mountain where none has plowed. Then he shall knead the soil with living water and shall make a body and begin to permutate the alef-bet of 221 gates, each limb separately, each limb with the corresponding letter mentioned in Sefer Yetzirah. And the alef-bets shall be permutated first, then afterward he shall permutate with the vowel—alef, bet, gimel, dalet—and always the letter of the divine name with them, and all the alef-bet. . . . Afterward he shall appoint bet and likewise gimel and each limb with the letter designated to it. He shall do this when he is pure. These are the 221 gates.

To control the golem, the creator writes one of the names of God on its forehead, or on a tablet under its tongue. This can then be erased or removed. Or the creator could write the word EMET (אמת, "truth") on its forehead. By erasing the first letter in EMET to form MET (מת, "dead") the creator would destroy the golem.

According to kabbalah, a golem can never disobey its creator.

Later golem stories aren't so sure. The most famous, "The Golem of Prague," tells the story of Rabbi Judah Loew, who creates a golem to defend Prague's Jewish ghetto against a pogrom. The golem did its job so well, killing people and scaring the bejeezus out of the ones it didn't kill, that Rabbi Loew destroyed it after securing a promise that Prague's Jews would be safe. Word is that the golem is stored in the attic of a synagogue in Prague, ready to be reanimated in time of need.

In other golem stories, the golem is dangerous or has magical abilities, including invisibility, a burning touch, and the power of summoning spirits.

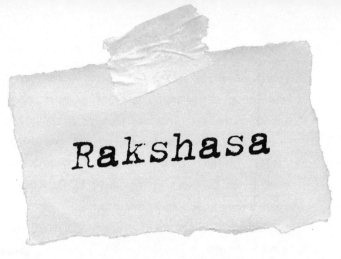

Rakshasa

Until we ran into one last year, the only thing we knew about *rakshasas* was that Kolchak the Night Stalker once ran into one. (Thanks to Ellen at the Roadhouse for fleshing things out. You other hunters will know what we're talking about.) *Rakshasas* come out of Hindu myth, where they are a kind of demon of chaos. They disrupt sacrifices, desecrate graves, eat people. Also, they can change shape, usually into human form or the shape of a large bird. And

that's not to mention the invisibility. Oh, and the ability to animate dead bodies.

The one we ran across was following the low-rent carnival circuit around the hinterlands, working as a blind knife-thrower. It lay pretty low most of the time, but every generation or so it would spend a couple of weeks taking the shape of a clown to beguile children into letting it into their houses.

Then it killed and ate the parents, and left one seriously traumatized kid behind. You can imagine how it made us even more than usually eager to put it down when we investigated and discovered all the nasty stuff it was up to. A *rakshasa* can be killed with a knife made of pure brass . . . if you can find it. Did we mention the invisibility?

GHOULS, REVENANTS, ET CETERA

he dead like to hang around graveyards, but hey, everybody's gotta get out sometimes, which means sometimes you get various revenants and ghouls and vampires screwing things up for us in the world of the living. The difference between a spirit and a revenant is that a revenant walks around in the same body it inhabited while it was alive. A spirit, if it's a real badass, might be able to ectoplasmically reconstitute its body, but only a revenant can motivate the genuine article. This is a distinction that's probably only important to us.

Folklore abounds with tales of the walking dead, and so do the accounts of historians, back when you could talk about stuff like this without having everyone in sight call for the guys in the white coats. We've seen just about every revenant story ever written down, and here's a little primer in the history of the dead who just won't stay dead. It begins with William of Newburgh, writing in England in the twelfth century:

> It would not be easy to believe that the corpses of the dead should sally (I know not by what agency) from their graves, and should wander about to the terror or destruction of the living, and again return to the tomb, which of its own accord spontaneously opened to receive them, did not frequent examples, occurring in our own times, suffice to establish this fact, to the truth of which there is abundant testimony. It would be strange if such things should have happened formerly, since we can find no evidence of them in the works of ancient authors,

whose vast labor it was to commit to writing every occurrence worthy of memory; for if they never neglected to register even events of moderate interest, how could they have suppressed a fact at once so amazing and horrible, supposing it to have happened in their day? Moreover, were I to write down all the instances of this kind which I have ascertained to have befallen in our times, the undertaking would be beyond measure laborious and troublesome.

William does write down a few, though. Dad transcribed some of them into his journal, and this one is interesting for the bit about the axe.

> As soon as this man was left alone in this place, the devil, imagining that he had found the right moment for breaking his courage, incontinently roused up his own chosen vessel, who appeared to have reposed longer than usual. Having beheld this from afar, he grew stiff with terror by reason of his being alone; but soon recovering his courage, and no place of refuge being at hand, he valiantly withstood the onset of the fiend, who came rushing upon him with a terrible noise, and he struck the axe which he wielded in his hand deep into his body. On receiving this wound, the monster groaned aloud, and turning his back, fled with a rapidity not at all inferior to that with which he had advanced, while the admirable man urged his flying foe from behind, and compelled him to seek his own tomb again; which opening of its own accord, and receiving its guest from the advance of the pursuer, immediately appeared to close again with the same facility. In the meantime, they who, impatient of the coldness of the night, had retreated to the fire ran up, though somewhat too late,

and, having heard what had happened, rendered needful assistance in digging up and removing from the midst of the tomb the accursed corpse at the earliest dawn. When they had divested it of the clay cast forth with it, they found the huge wound it had received, and a great quantity of gore which had flowed from it in the sepulchre; and so having carried it away beyond the walls of the monastery and burnt it, they scattered the ashes to the winds.

Another case from 1591 involves a *nachzehrer*, the name for revenants used in northern Germany. Known as the case of the shoemaker of Silesia, it starts off with a family trying to cover up a suicide. The truth gets out, though, because the *corpse* gets out, and terrorizes the citizens of Breslau for eight months. We'll pick it up when the townspeople are starting to get suspicious about the widow's claim that her husband had a stroke, when in fact he'd cut his own throat (or had he?):

In the meantime a ghost appeared now and again, in just such a form as the shoemaker had in his lifetime, and during the day as well as at night. It scared many people through its very form, awakened others with noises, oppressed others, and others it vexed in other ways, so that early in the morning one heard talk everywhere about the ghost. But the more the ghost appeared, the less the relatives wanted to celebrate. They went to the president of the court and said that too much credence was being placed in the people's unfounded rumors, the honorable man was being abused in his grave, and they found themselves obliged to take the matter to the kaiser. But now that the matter actually brought about a prohibition, the state of haunting became even worse. For the ghost was there right after sundown, and since no one was free of it, everyone looked around constantly for it. The ones most bothered were those who wanted to rest after heavy work; often it came to their bed, often it actually lay down in it and was like to smother the people. Indeed, it squeezed them so hard that—not without astonishment—people could see the marks left by its fingers, so that one could easily judge the so-called stroke. In this manner the people, who were fearful in any case, became yet more fearful, so they did not remain longer in their houses, but sought for more secure places. Most of them, not secure in their bedchamber, stayed in the rooms, after bringing many others in, so that their fear was dispersed by the crowd. Nonetheless, although they all waked with burning lights, the ghost came anyway. Often everyone saw it, but often just a few, of whom it always harassed some.

Eventually, they can't stand it, and they open the coffin, discovering that the shoemaker looks pretty damn good for a guy who's been dead eight months. In fact, the body showed zero signs of decomposition. Didn't even stink. So they take drastic action, placing the shoemaker's body on a bier where it was guarded day and night. Does this stop the hauntings? Hardly.

The exhumation did not help: the ghost, which they had hoped to banish by this means, caused still more unrest. The corpse was laid under the gallows, but this didn't help either, for the ghost then raged so cruelly that one cannot describe it. But now, as the ghost was raging so terribly and thereby causing great inconvenience to many citizens as well as his good friends, the widow went to the council and said that she would admit everything, they could deal with her former husband with all strictness. But in the short time from April 24 to May 7, the body had grown much fuller of flesh, which everyone could see who remembered how it had looked before. Whereupon, on the seventh, the council had the hangman take the corpse out of the other grave. Then its head was cut off, its hands and feet dismembered, after which the back was cut open and the heart taken out, which looked as good as that of a freshly slaughtered calf. Everything togther was burned on a pyre built up of seven *klafters* of wood and of many pitch rings. But so that no one would gather the ashes or the bones and keep them for sorcery, as tends to happen otherwise, the guards were not allowed to let anyone near. Early in the morning, when the stack of wood had burned up, the ashes, in a sack, were thrown into the flowing water, whereupon, through God's help, the ghost stayed away and was never seen again.

It's all here: the coverup after the death, the family slowly realizing that the lie is going to come back to haunt them (literally), and at last the emergence of the truth. The shoemaker of Silesia is a blueprint for lots of revenants that came after him, because people never change, either before or after they die.

You'll often see people using the words "revenant" and "ghoul" as if they're the same. They're not. You got your different risen-from-the-dead varieties, and a ghoul is just one flavor. The categories are kind of fluid, get it? That's why, for us, even vampires could be considered a subcategory of revenant, because they're not demons and they're not spirits. Process of elimination. Plus, they go around in their own bodies, the ones they had back when they were ordinary folk who never craved the sweet taste of type O neg. We've tangled with them twice, and even let them go once—which didn't sit too well with some other hunters.

Anyway, on to the ghouls.

Ghoul

Where does the word "ghoul" come from? Before it came to be applied to any random sicko or serial killer, it went all the way back to the medieval Arabic *ghul*, which meant a kind of demon. Specifically a kind of demon that lived in graveyards and was the offspring of Iblis, a jinn roughly corresponding to Satan (in fact, later known as al-Shaitan). Like other demons, Iblis gets jonesing for human women once in a while—well, all the time—and every time he scores, that's one more *ghul* in the world. Iblis was allowed to roam the earth, unlike his Judeo-Christian counterpart, because Allah wanted to test people by allowing someone to put wicked ideas into their heads. Which seems like overkill to us, since as far as we've been able to tell, people are more than capable of coming up with wicked ideas on their own.

But "demon" doesn't mean the same thing in this context as it does when we're talking about Christian demonology, either. We're not going to go all the way into it, but trust us when we say that your average ghoul or revenant, though a serious obstacle to our pursuit of happiness, is not the same kind of demon we mean when we talk about the Yellow-Eyed Son of a Bitch. *Ghul* also means a kind of desert-dwelling shapeshifter, often assuming the guise of a hyena, that lures travelers off paths so it can eat them. It's especially fond of children and will dig up graves to eat the dead.

Here's a good example, from *Histoire curieuse et pittoresque des sorciers*, as edited by Fornari:

There lived at Baghdad an aged merchant who had grown wealthy in his business, and who had an only son to whom he was tenderly attached. He resolved to marry him to the daughter of another merchant, a girl of considerable fortune, but without any personal attractions. Abul-Hassan, the merchant's son, on being shown the portrait of the lady, requested his father to delay the marriage till he could reconcile his mind to it. Instead, however, of doing this, he fell in love with another girl, the daughter of a sage, and he gave his father no peace till he consented to the marriage with the object of his affections. The old man stood out as long as he could, but finding that his son was bent on acquiring the hand of the fair Nadilla, and was equally resolute not to accept the rich and ugly lady, he did what most fathers, under such circumstances, are constrained to do, he acquiesced.

The wedding took place with great pomp and ceremony, and a happy honeymoon ensued, which might have been happier but for one little circumstance which led to very serious consequences.

Abul-Hassan noticed that his bride quitted the nuptial couch as soon as she thought her husband was asleep, and did not return to it, till an hour before dawn.

Filled with curiosity, Hassan one night feigned sleep, and saw his wife rise and leave the room as usual. He followed cautiously, and saw her enter a cemetery. By the straggling moonbeams he beheld her go into a tomb; he stepped in after her.

The scene within was horrible. A party of ghouls were assembled with the spoils of the graves they had violated, and were feasting on the flesh of the long-buried corpses. His own wife, who, by the way, never touched supper at home, played no inconsiderable part in the hideous banquet.

As soon as he could safely escape, Abul-Hassan stole back to his bed.

He said nothing to his bride till next evening when supper was laid, and she declined to eat; then he insisted on her partaking, and when she positively refused, he exclaimed wrathfully, "Yes, you keep your appetite for your feast with the ghouls!" Nadilla was silent; she turned pale and trembled, and without a word sought her bed. At midnight she rose, fell on her husband with her nails and teeth, tore his throat, and having opened a vein, attempted to suck his blood; but Abul-Hassan springing to his feet threw her down, and with a blow killed her. She was buried the next day.

Three days after, at midnight, she reappeared, attacked her husband again, and again attempted to suck his blood. He fled from her, and on the morrow opened her tomb, burned her to ashes, and cast them into the Tigris.

The exhuming and burning of a corpse has been one of the standard revenant-disposal measures as long as there have been revenants. Variations spring up—boy, do they spring up—but fire is a standby. We swear by it. Even when we've wasted something by other means, we burn whatever there is to burn, just to make sure.

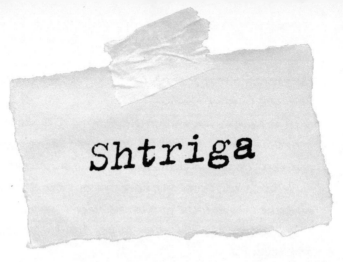

Shtriga

Folklore abounds with tales of creatures that were once human, but became otherwise due to some kind of magic or supernatural phenomenon. The *wendigo* is one, the loup-garou is another. And then there's the *shtriga*. You can go all the way back to the ancients and find records of something they called the *strix*, which they described as a kind of creature that as punishment for cannibalism became deformed—again like the *wendigo*—and turned into a kind of night-flyer perceived by the Romans as, in the words of Antoninus Liberalis, "a harbinger of war and civil strife to men." Hopefully by now you're getting the picture that people eating people is never a good move.

By the Middle Ages, the *shtriga* was described as a witch, but everything was described as a witch in the Middle Ages. Other descriptions of it link it with the Romanian *strigoi*, which is a kind of vampire. That's not quite accurate, either. Our take on it is that the *shtriga* is a revenant, a walking undead in a body that should have died a long time ago. It may not technically be dead, but it feeds on the *spiritus vitae*, draining the life force of its victims. That's what keeps it going. Usually it attacks children, working its way through all of the siblings in a family before moving on to the next.

The *shtriga* is one of the few monsters that it took us Winchesters two full hunts to bring down, because the first time we met it, we were little kids. That was in Fort Douglas, Wisconsin. While Dad was hunting it, the *shtriga* came after us—and we think he knew something was going to happen, because right when it started to get down to business, there he came busting through the door with guns blazing. He hit it, but didn't kill it, so that's why we ended up in Fitchburg, just down the road from Fort Douglas, seventeen years later.

We finished the job. The *shtriga* is vulnerable only when it's feeding, and then only to consecrated cold iron. We tracked it, waited until we knew which kid it was going after next, and then put it down.

You'd think there would have been something in Dad's journal about the *shtriga*, but there isn't, and we're guessing it's because Dad knew we'd run across it again, and he knew Dean would remember. No sense rubbing his face in it. Dean's always blamed himself for not drawing down on it then, but he was ten. There are some things ten-year-olds shouldn't have to do. Facing down a thousand-year-old Albanian revenant is one of them.

Draugr/ Draug

The *draugr* haunted the graves of dead Vikings, but also returned from the dead to cause death and chaos in settled villages; in *Eyrbyggja saga*, a *draugr* named Thorolf kills so many people that the entire valley it haunts is abandoned. *Draugrs* are also mentioned in *Laxdaela saga* and, of course, *Grettir's saga*. If haunting the grave of a wealthy man, the *draugr* would guard the treasure and hunt down any man who stole from the tomb. Hugely strong and deathly pallid, the *draugr* could also change its size, and as if that wasn't bad enough, it was often immune to ordinary weapons wielded by ordinary men. It usually took a hero to dispatch a *draugr*, which easily killed with brute force before eating its victims and drinking their blood. Some tales have the *draugr* leaving its grave as a plume of smoke before assuming humanoid shape. Heroes in the sagas frequently confront the *draugr* without weapons, wrestling it into submission. Not always, though: Grettir, after an exhausting fight that wrecks the hall where it begins, kills the *draugr* known as Glam with a blow from his sword.

Unless the *draugr's* body was disposed of in some drastic way, it could come back. Like some accounts of the disposal of the bodies of revenants, the Icelandic sagas suggest that the best way of getting rid of a *draugr* for good is to decapitate it, burn it, and then pour the ashes into the sea.

Eyrbyggja saga: Thorir Wood-Leg kills several men, who then go all undead. Cut to the sea, where six men die and then return to the farm, equally undead and dripping wet. The two sets of revenants fight, and then the *draugr* Thorolf kills so many that his valley is evacuated.

Laxdaela saga: Regarding the *draugr* named Killer-Hrapp, "Difficult as he had been to deal with during his life, he was now very much worse after death, for his corpse would not rest in its grave."

Some *draugrs* were able to leave their dwelling place, the burial mound, and visit the living during the night. Such visits were universally horrible events, often ended in death for one or more of the living, and warranted the exhumation of the *draugr*'s tomb by a hero.

Some *draugrs*, known as *haugbui*, haunted grave sites only and left mortals alone unless their graves were violated or approached too closely.

The *draugr* had a crafty cousin known as the *draug*, which is more closely identified with sea life. *Draugs* were known to make sailors slip dangerously on wet rocks as they came ashore—this variety is known as the *gleip*—and although they usually have a human appearance, there are some major differences. Sometimes the *draug*'s head is composed of seaweed; other times it doesn't have a head at all. (And if you're supposed to decapitate revenants, what do you do with the headless ones?)

Draug sometimes swim alongside boats, waiting for the chance to dupe sailors into slipping on the rocks. Some tales say they can change shape to appear as seaweed or slippery stones. Unless a sailor spits on one of these stones, stepping on it will be fatal. Another malevolent use of the stone shape is when sailors unknowingly bring a *draug* aboard a ship in the guise of a stone. Once the ship sails, the *draug* returns to its natural shape, causing a shift in weight that capsizes the ship.

In addition to being major trouble on their own, *draugs* are death omens. Seeing or hearing one is assumed to be an indication that tragedy is just around the corner. We've never run into one, but just knowing about them is enough to make us want to stay off boats. And out of Scandinavia.

Vampire

The first time we ever fought vampires was when we were looking for a gun that shot magic bullets.

No, really.

Samuel Colt once made a gun and thirteen magic bullets that could kill anything with a single shot. Dad found out about it, and we realized that we finally had our kryptonite for the Yellow-Eyed Bastard. For the first time, we were on his trail and we had a line on a weapon that could make a difference. If we had to go through a nest of vampires to get that gun, we'd do it. And we did.

We were a little surprised even to find vampires, since Dad had been under the impression that a hunter buddy of his, Daniel Elkins, had killed the last remaining North American vampire. Guess Elkins had missed some, though, because we found plenty. And we weren't sure what we were getting into, because the folklore about vampires is so vast and contradictory that it's tough to sort out what's really going to work from what some medieval monk thought he heard the local sexton say over a morning glass of sour wine.

Here's a little background on vampires, before we get back to the Colt.

As near as anyone can tell, the first English use of the word "vampire" happens in about 1734, in *The Travels of Three English Gentlemen*, now known only as part of volume four of the 1745 *Harleian*

Miscellany: "We must not omit Observing here, that our Landlord seems to pay some regard to what Baron Valvasor has related of the Vampyres, said to infest some Parts of this Country. These Vampyres are supposed to be the Bodies of deceased Persons, animated by evil Spirits, which come out of the Graves, in the Night-time, suck the Blood of many of the Living, and thereby destroy them."

This is around the same time as the first great vampire scares in continental Europe, the most famous of which was an account of the post-death activities of one Peter Plogojowitz in 1725. The entire report, as filed by a local bureaucrat, goes like this:

> After a subject by the name of Peter Plogojowitz had died, ten weeks past—he lived in the village of Kisilova, in the Rahm district [of Serbia]—and had been buried according to the Raetzin custom, it had been revealed that in this same village of Kisilova, within a week, nine people, both old and young, died also, after suffering a twenty-four-hour illness. And they said publicly, while they were yet alive, but on their death-bed, that the above-mentioned Peter Plogojowitz, who had died ten weeks earlier, had come to them in their sleep, laid himself on them, so that they would have to give up the ghost. The other subjects were very distressed and strengthened even more in such beliefs by the fact that the dead Peter Plogojowitz's wife, after saying her husband had come to her and demanded his *opanki*, or shoes, had left the village of Kisilova and gone to another.
>
> And since with such people (which they call vampires) various signs are to be seen—that is, the body undecomposed, the skin, hair, beard, and nails growing—the subjects resolved unanimously to open the grave of Peter Plogojowitz and to see if such above-mentioned signs were really to be found on him. To this end they came here to me and, telling of these events, asked me and the local pope, or the parish priest, to be present at the viewing. And although I at first disapproved, telling them that the praiseworthy administration should first be dutifully and humbly informed, and its exalted opinion about this should be

heard, they did not want to accommodate themselves to this at all, but rather gave this short answer: I could do what I want, but if I could not accord them the viewing and the legal recognition to deal with the body according to their custom, they would have to leave house and home, because by the time a gracious resolution was received from Belgrade, perhaps the entire village—and this was already supposed to have happened once before under the Turks—could be destroyed by such an evil spirit, and they did not want to wait for this.

Since I could not hold such people from the resolution they had made, either with good words or with threats, I went to the village of Kisilova, taking along the Gradisk pope, and viewed the body of Peter Plogojowitz, just exhumed, finding, in accordance with thorough thoughtfulness, that first of all I did not detect the slightest odor that is otherwise characteristic of the dead, and the body, except for the nose, which was somewhat fallen away, was completely fresh. The hair and beard—even the nails, of which the old ones had fallen away—had grown on him; the old skin, which was somewhat whitish, had peeled away, and a new fresh one had emerged under it. The face, hands, and feet, and the whole body were so constituted, that they could not have been more complete in his lifetime. Not without astonishment, I saw some fresh blood in his mouth, which, according to the common observation, he had sucked from the people killed by him. In short, all the indications were present that such people (as remarked above) are said to have.

After both the pope and I had seen this spectacle, while the people grew more outraged than distressed, all the subjects, with great speed, sharpened a stake—in order to pierce the corpse of the deceased with it—and put this at his heart, whereupon, as he was pierced, not only did much blood, completely fresh, flow also through his ears and mouth, but still other wild signs (which I pass by out of high respect) took place.

Finally, according to their usual practice, they burned the often-mentioned body, *in hoc casu,* to ashes, of which I inform the most laudable Administration, and at the same time would like to request, obediently and humbly, that if a mistake was made in this matter, such is to be attributed not to me but to the rabble, who were beside themselves with fear.

Around the same time, another vampire, this one named Arnod Paole, was stirring up trouble in his hometown of Medvegia, Serbia. Five years after his death, Medvegia was suddenly under siege, with seventeen people dead in less than three months. The emperor of Austria himself, Charles VI, decreed that an inquiry was needed. The results of the inquiry, called *Visum et Repertum* and signed by a number of military officers, including a regimental field surgeon, went something like this:

After it had been reported that in the village of Medvegia the so-called vampires had killed some people by sucking their blood, I was, by high decree of a local Honorable Supreme Command, sent there to investigate the matter thoroughly along with officers detailed for that purpose and two subordinate medical officers, and therefore carried out and heard the present inquiry in the company of the captain of the Stallath Company of *haiduks*, Gorschiz Hadnack, the standard-bearer and the oldest *haiduk* of the village, as follows: who unanimously recounted that about five years ago a local *haiduk* by the name of Arnod Paole broke his neck in a fall from a haywagon. This man had during his lifetime often revealed that, near Gossowa in Turkish Serbia, he had been troubled by a vampire, wherefore he had eaten from the earth of the vampire's grave and had smeared himself with the vampire's blood, in order to be free from the vexation he had suffered. In 20 or 30 days after his death some people complained that they were being bothered by this same Arnod Paole; and in fact four people were killed by him.

In order to end this evil, they dug up this Arnod Paole 40 days after his death—this on the advice of Hadnack, who had been present at such events before; and they found that he was quite complete and undecayed, and that fresh blood had flowed from his eyes, nose, mouth, and ears; that the shirt, the covering, and the coffin were completely bloody; that the old nails on his hands and feet, along with the skin, had fallen off, and that new ones had grown; and since they saw from this that he was a true vampire, they drove a stake through his heart, according to their custom, whereby he gave an audible groan and bled copiously.

Thereupon they burned the body the same day to ashes and threw these into the grave. These people say further that all those who were tormented and killed by the vampire must themselves become vampires. Therefore they disinterred the above-mentioned four people in the same way. Then they also add that this Arnod Paole attacked not only the people but also the cattle, and sucked out their blood. And since the people used the flesh of such cattle, it appears that some vampires are again present here, inasmuch as, in a period of three months, 17 young and old people died, among them some who, with no previous illness, died in two or at the most three days. In addition, the *haiduk* Jowiza reports that his step-daughter, by the name of Stanacka, lay down to sleep 15 days ago, fresh and healthy, but at midnight she started up out of her sleep with a terrible cry, fearful and trembling, and complained that she had been throttled by the son of a *haiduk* by the name of Milloe, who had died nine weeks earlier, whereupon she had experienced a great pain in the chest and became worse hour by hour, until finally she died on the third day.

At this we went the same afternoon to the graveyard, along with the oftenmentioned oldest *haiduks* of the village, in order to cause the suspicious graves to be opened and to examine the bodies in them, whereby, after all of them had been dissected, there was found:

1. A woman by the name of Stana, 20 years old, who had died in childbirth two months ago, after a three-day illness, and who had herself said, before her death, that she had painted herself with the blood of a vampire, wherefore both she and her child—which had died right after birth and because of a careless burial had been half eaten by the dogs—must also become vampires. She was quite complete and undecayed. After the opening of the body there was found in the *cavitate pectoris* a quantity of fresh extravascular blood. The vessels of the arteries and veins, like the *ventriculis ortis*, were not, as is usual, filled with coagulated blood, and the whole viscera, that is, the lung, liver, stomach, spleen, and intestines were quite fresh as they would be in a healthy person. The uterus was however quite enlarged and very inflamed externally, for the placenta and lochia had remained in place, wherefore the same was in complete putredine. The skin on her hands and feet, along with the old nails, fell away on their

own, but on the other hand completely new nails were evident, along with a fresh and vivid skin.

2. There was a woman by the name of Miliza (60 years old), who had died after a three-month sickness and had been buried 90-some days earlier. In the chest much liquid blood was found; and the other viscera were, like those mentioned before, in a good condition. During her dissection, all the *haiduks* who were standing around marveled greatly at her plumpness and perfect body, uniformly stating that they had known the woman well, from her youth, and that she had, throughout her life, looked and been very lean and dried up, and they emphasized that she had come to this surprising plumpness in the grave. They also said that it was she who started the vampires this time, because she had eaten of the flesh of those sheep that had been killed by the previous vampires.

3. There was an eight-day-old child which had lain in the grave for 90 days and was similarly in a condition of vampirism.

4. The son of a *haiduk*, 16 years old, was dug up, having lain in the earth for nine weeks, after he had died from a three-day illness, and was found like the other vampires.

5. Joachim, also the son of a *haiduk*, 17 years old; had died after a three-day illness. He had been buried eight weeks and four days and, on being dissected, was found in similar condition.

6. A woman by the name of Ruscha who had died after a ten-day illness and had been buried six weeks previous, in whom there was much fresh blood not only in the chest but also in *fundo ventriculi*. The same showed itself in her child, which was 18 days old and had died five weeks previously.

7. No less did a girl ten years of age, who had died two months previously, find herself in the above-mentioned condition, quite complete and undecayed, and had much fresh blood in her chest.

8. They caused the wife of the Hadnack to be dug up, along with her child. She had died seven weeks previously, her child—who was eight weeks old—21 days previously, and it was found that both mother and child were completely decomposed, although earth and grave were like those of the vampires lying nearby.

9. A servant of the local corporal of the *haiduk,* by the name of Rhade, 21 years old, died after a three-month-long illness, and after a five week burial was found completely decomposed.

10. The wife of the local *bariactar,* along with her child, having died five weeks previously, were also completely decomposed.

11. With Stanche, a local *haiduk,* 60 years old, who had died six weeks previously, I noticed a profuse liquid blood, like the others, in the chest and stomach. The entire body was in the oft-named condition of vampirism.

12. Milloe, a *haiduk,* 25 years old, who had lain for six weeks in the earth, also was found in the condition of vampirism mentioned.

13. Stanoika, the wife of a *haiduk,* 20 years old, died after a three-day illness and had been buried 18 days previously. In the dissection I found that she was in her countenance quite red and of a vivid color, and, as was mentioned above, she had been throttled, at midnight, by Milloe, the son of the *haiduk,* and there was also to be seen, on the right side under the ear, a bloodshot blue mark, the length of a finger. As she was being taken out of the grave, a quantity of fresh blood flowed from her nose. With the dissection I found, as mentioned often already, a regular fragrant fresh bleeding, not only in the chest cavity, but also in *ventriculo cordis.* All the viscera found themselves in a completely good and healthy condition. The hypodermis of the entire body, along with the fresh nails of the hands and feet, was as though completely fresh.

After the examination had taken place, the heads of the vampires were cut off by the local gypsies and burned along with the bodies, and then the ashes were thrown into the river Morava. The decomposed bodies, however, were laid back into their own graves. Which I attest along with those assistant medical officers provided for me. *Actum ut supra:*

> (L.S.) *Johannes Fluchinger, Regimental Medical Officer of the Foot Regiment of the Honorable B. Fürstenbusch.*

> (L.S.) *J. H. Sigel, Medical Officer of the Honorable Morall Regiment.*

> (L.S.) *Johann Friedrich Baumgarten, Medical Officer of the Foot Regiment of the Honorable B. Fürstenbusch.*

The undersigned attest herewith that all which the Regimental
Medical Officer of the Foot Regiment of the Honorable
B. Fürstenbusch has observed in the matter of vampires—along
with both medical officers who signed with him—is in every way
truthful and has been undertaken, observed, and examined in
our own presence. In confirmation thereof is our signature in
our own hand, of our making, Belgrade, January 26, 1732.

(L.S.) Büttener, Lieutenant Colonel of the Honorable Alexandrian
Regiment.

(L.S.) J. H. von Lindenfels, Officer of the Honorable Alexandrian
Regiment.

But that wasn't the beginning of Europe's vampire troubles. As far back as the sixteenth century, various local governments in Europe were handing out bounties for the hunting and killing of vampires and loups-garou.

Oh, and the mirror thing? Near as we can tell, that's one of Bram Stoker's inventions. Same with turning into mist and the rest of it. Vampires, when you get right down to it, are pretty simple. "Crosses won't repel them, and sunlight won't kill them," Dad said— although they do sunburn wicked fast and don't like to be outside in broad daylight. And we found out that they need to drink blood to survive and can only be killed by beheading, although dead man's blood will poison them and slow them down. Oh, and they can be killed by a bullet from the magic Colt. Anywho, here's what happened:

We were in Nebraska, looking around for something interesting to kill, when we ran across a newspaper obit about Daniel Elkins being killed. The name rang a bell, and there it was in Dad's journal. So we headed to Manning, Colorado, to check it out, and found a ring of salt around the front entrance to the house. First clue: Elkins knew something about something.

Then we ran into Dad, who had come for the same reason we had. But he had another reason, which was that he was looking for the Colt. We figured out that Elkins had been keeping it, which meant that whatever had gotten him, that was who we had to take the gun from. Elkins's journal was a trove of information on vampires: they nest in small groups, eight to ten, and send out individuals or smaller groups to hunt. Victims are taken to the nest, where they're kept alive for as long as the vampires can restrain themselves.

No way to live, if you ask us. And for their victims, no way to die. And in this case, it was worse, because these vampires had killed a hunter. That made it a grudge match, especially for Dad. Elkins was one of the first to show him the ropes, introduce him around to other hunters. Now Elkins was gone, and there were some vampires who had to pay.

That first hunt, we killed us some vampires—arrows dipped in dead man's blood to slow them down, and machetes for the finish work. Along the way, we saved a few people from becoming a permanent lunch—and we got the Colt. Although we had to waste one bullet on the leader of that nest, a tough guy who called himself Luther.

The other thing we did was become a family again. Winchester and Sons, at your service—if only for a while.

The next time we saw vampires, Dad was dead.

And as if that wasn't enough of a shock, the vampires weren't all that bad.

This was in Red Lodge, Montana, after we'd lost the Colt, and we'd lost Dad, and we were starting to get the feeling that war—the Demon War—was really on the horizon. In other words, things were pretty freakin' crappy. We'd heard about a couple of decapitation murders and some cattle mutilations happening out in the boonies of Montana, and with nothing better to do, we headed up to Big Sky Country.

A little note on cattle mutilation, since that was one of the things that first alerted us to the strange doings in Red Lodge. Cattle mutilation is not performed by little green men. Or little gray aliens. Cattle mutilation is either performed by sicko human beings, of whom there are plenty, or it's a product of people wanting to see what isn't there. They get our attention because sometimes people who mutilate cattle are up to other things as well, like for example throwing on cheesy black robes and chanting "Hail Satan" while performing human sacrifices. But aliens? Somehow we doubt they'd travel a hundred billion miles just to go Mengele on a bunch of cows. So before you start in on that story about those crazy lights you saw in the sky that one night you were barbecuing on the back porch? We should tell you: UFO people are crazy. *I want to believe*—fine. Believe. Do whatever. But there's no such thing as UFOs. It always turns out to be something else. A hoax or a weather balloon—or something up our alley. Something supernatural.

First thing that happened in Red Lodge was that we alienated the sheriff, but that's practically standard operating procedure. The second thing was that we wormed ourselves into the morgue under false pretenses to check out the dead girl with the detached head. That's when we discovered that the dead girl had been a vampire.

Okay, we thought. This is interesting. Maybe six months before, we'd been convinced that vampires were as mythical as unicorns, or if not mythical, then extinct. The dodo birds of the revenant world. Now we'd seen them once and had real, dead evidence of another nest.

The third thing that happened was that we met Gordon Walker.

We learned a lot from Gordon. We learned that there's an etiquette among hunters, which we'd never known because the Winchesters had always hunted on their own. Later, when we'd met Bobby Singer and Ellen and Jo and some others, we realized that there was this whole subculture of unrecognized heroes out there. Risking their lives every day to eliminate threats that most people wouldn't believe in, even when the fangs were sinking into their throats. Speaking of fangs, that's what Gordon called vampires. He seemed to think there were a lot of them, which told us something else about hunters; they don't communicate too well. Daniel Elkins and Dad had thought the vampires were gone, but here was Gordon acting like they were behind every tree.

Another thing we learned from Gordon was that a hunter doesn't want to share a hunt. At least he didn't. But Gordon wasn't normal, even for a hunter.

What is normal for a hunter? They—*we*—tend to be cut off from most normal societal institutions like job and family. They also tend to be in this line of work for personal reasons. Maybe some kind of supernatural baddie killed someone close to them, which can make a person a bit single-minded. Obsessive, even. This we understand. Gordon was a little different, though. He liked the work. We take pride in doing our job well, and take satisfaction from reducing the amount of evil in the world, but Gordon liked the work. A little *too* much.

How do we know this? Because we found out during the course of investigating the Red Lodge situation. Turned out that the vampires were responsible for the cattle mutilations, and Gordon was responsible for the decapitations. Of the vampires. Who weren't feeding on people because they were sick of being hunted.

Whoa.

Vampires not feeding on people? Doing the right thing by sublimating their desire for human blood and killing cattle instead? And a hunter killing things that—we had to swallow hard to admit this—weren't evil?

This was one of those more-things-in-heaven-and-earth moments. You just never know what you're going to find when you go on a job.

At first it was pretty hard to believe, even though Sam had first-hand evidence: the vampires had kidnapped him and then let him go, just to prove their point. Gordon definitely wasn't buying it, and then we caught up with him torturing one of the vampires to force her to reveal the location of the others. That's when we really knew that in Gordon, that hunter instinct had burned through his sense of right and wrong. He had his reasons: vampires had attacked him in his home when he was just a teenager. Beat the crap out of him and taken his sister. Turned her.

So he left home, learned how to track and kill vampires, and hunted down his sister. Or, in his words, the monster who *used to be* his sister. And he killed her.

That's enough to make anyone a little dark. But a hunter who starts to like torture? He isn't all that far from flipping over and becoming a tool of exactly the forces we're all trying to exterminate. When you begin to enjoy inflicting pain—which isn't the same as the grim satisfaction you take from eliminating evil—you've turned into something else. Something bad—maybe just as bad as the things you hunt. You look in the abyss, the abyss looks back.

We faced off with Gordon over this and ended up doing two things we never in our lives imagined we'd do. One, we got in a serious no-quarter fight with another hunter; two, we let the vampires go.

Next time might be different (the next time with Gordon sure was, but more about that later). It's not like we're going to go around assuming the next vampire nest we run into will be full of vegetarians. Anything that preys on humans is our target, and our best guess is that the next time we find a vampire, it'll be sucking the blood out of people instead of cows. In which case we'll take its head and move along to the next thing.

And everything will be back to normal.

Zombie

It took us a long time to run across a real walking zombie. You'd think it would have happened sooner, given all the other kinds of strange beings we've seen, but no. Twenty years on the hunt, give or take, and finally we get our first zombie. She was cute, too, until she started killing people.

The thing about zombie and revenant lore is that there's so much of it that you almost can't sort through and find out what's really true. Everybody's seen *Night of the Living Dead*, but trust us: as far as we know, getting bitten by a zombie doesn't turn you into one. It might get you dead, though. And anyway, most zombies don't bite. Some of the other ghoulish revenants do, but we're talking about zombies here.

The word itself comes from *nzambi*, used in Bantu languages to talk about spirits of dead people or ancestors. In some West African religions, Nzambi is also the name of a creator god, the kind who presided over creation and then stepped back to watch things unfold. On its way to the West Indies, the word came to be used for the prototypical Haitian zombie, famous from voodoo lore.

Creation of a zombie in this tradition involves a combination of sorcery and nerve poison extracted from the pufferfish. The *bokor* (more about them when we talk about witchcraft) who concocts the potion just has to sit and wait once it's administered. The victim suffers from increasing lethargy and finally lapses into a state virtually indistinguishable from death. Often the victim is buried, and the *bokor* can then exhume him and put him to work. Haitian history is full of zombies—hell, the big sugar companies all used them as an uncomplaining workforce. The only problem is that if you feed one of these zombies salt or meat, it will be triggered to recognize its state and will shuffle off to the grave. (There's salt again.)

But back to our zombie. She was reanimated by a deft bit of Greek necromancy, which is more often a tradition of communicating with the dead and using them for divination. Even Odysseus got up to this in Book XI of *The Odyssey*, which interested Dad enough that he copied the relevant passage into his journal.

> Here Perimedes and Eurylochus held the victims, while I drew my sword and dug the trench a cubit each way. I made a drink-offering to all the dead, first with honey and milk, then with wine, and thirdly with water, and I sprinkled white barley meal over the whole, praying earnestly to the poor feckless ghosts, and promising them that when I got back to Ithaca I would sacrifice a barren heifer for them, the best I had, and would load the pyre with good things. I also particularly promised that Tiresias should have a black sheep to himself, the best in all my flocks. When I had prayed sufficiently to the dead, I cut the throats of the two sheep and let the blood run into the trench, whereon the ghosts came trooping up from Erebus—brides, young bachelors, old men worn out with toil, maids who had been crossed in love, and brave men who had been killed in battle, with their armor still smirched with blood; they came from every quarter and flitted round the trench with a strange

kind of screaming sound that made me turn pale with fear. When I saw them coming I told the men to be quick and flay the carcasses of the two dead sheep and make burnt offerings of them, and at the same time to repeat prayers to Hades and to Persephone; but I sat where I was with my sword drawn and would not let the poor feckless ghosts come near the blood till Tiresias should have answered my questions.

This is the standard kind of Greek necromancy, although some of the more powerful practitioners added *katabasis* to their repertoires. In *katabasis*, a spirit projection of the necromancer travels to the underworld. A related practice, known as *katadesmoi*, is one of the more dangerous things you can do. A spirit is summoned and the necromancer imposes a quest on it. As you can imagine, most spirits aren't thrilled with the idea, and few things can go wrong faster than *katadesmoi*.

Another thing you can do in various necromantic practices, of course, is take *katadesmoi* one step further and fix your summoned spirit inside a body. Agrippa's *Three Books of Occult Philosophy* mentions this, and it's a staple of occult tradition. Dad's take on it is pretty sharp:

Death is the separation of the soul from the body. The creation of a zombie is the rebinding of body and soul via necromancy. The animated body can move, speak, even think, but it still can't outrun physical decay. Zombies don't last very long, and the more able they are to think, the more they suffer from the same derangement that eventually gets any spirit that's been

Yep, this is exactly what happened with our zombie. A young woman died in a car crash while arguing with her cheating boyfriend on her cell phone. That's a recipe for an angry spirit right there, but this time the dead girl had an admirer who just happened to know a little bit about Greek necromancy from his studies with a prominent classics professor. He brought the girl back for a little forbidden love and stood by while she killed the boyfriend and then tried to get the girl the boyfriend had cheated with. We stepped in there and plugged her with silver bullets, but they didn't take her down. Then her loverboy necromancer rubbed her the wrong way and she killed him, too.

Meanwhile, we were trying to figure out what to do with her. She'd already survived silver bullets, and she'd fallen on a pair of scissors while trying to kill her roommate, so we were at a loss.

How to Kill a Zombie/ Revenant

We started digging around in the lore regarding revenants of all sorts, not just your classic zombie. How the hell do you keep them in their coffins? Here's what we found: the lore says everything. It all overlaps or conflicts. You can be told to cut out the heart, soak it in wine, and put it back; or drive needles into the feet; or cut off the head, hands, and feet before burying everything at a crossroads; burn the body and throw the ashes in running water; or—our personal favorite—rely on the local population of wolves or wild dogs to dig the revenant out of its grave and tear it apart. But these are the most common ones:

Cut the Head Off and Put It Between the Feet

You find this one all over, but the best story is from the Icelandic tale *Grettir's saga*, after Grettir kills the *draugr* called Glam.

> When the thrall had spoken the faintness which had come over Grettir left him. He drew his short sword, cut off Glam's head, and laid it between his thighs. Then the *bondi* came out, having put on his clothes while Glam was speaking, but he did not venture to come near until he was dead. Thorhall praised God and thanked Grettir warmly for having laid this unclean spirit. Then they set to work and burned Glam to cold cinders, bound the ashes in a skin, and buried them in a place far away from the haunts of man or beast.

Other cases of this treatment of revenants are reported as recently as 1913, which probably means it's still happening.

Burn the Body

At the mouth of the river Tweed, and in the jurisdiction of the king of Scotland, there stands a noble city which is called Berwick. In this town a certain man, very wealthy, but as it afterwards appeared a great rogue, having been buried, after his death sallied forth (by the contrivance, as it is believed, of Satan) out of his grave by night, and was borne hither and thither, pursued by a pack of dogs with loud barkings; thus striking great terror into the neighbors, and returning to his tomb before daylight. After this had continued for several days, and no one dared to be found out of doors after dusk—for each dreaded an encounter with this deadly monster—the higher and middle classes of the people held a necessary investigation into what was requisite to be done; the more simple among them fearing, in the event of negligence, to be soundly beaten by this prodigy of the grave; but the wiser shrewdly concluding that were a remedy further delayed, the atmosphere, infected and corrupted by the constant whirlings through it of the pestiferous corpse, would engender disease and death to a great extent; the necessity of providing against which was shown by frequent examples in similar cases. They, therefore, procured ten young men renowned for boldness, who were to dig up the horrible carcass, and, having cut it limb from limb, reduce it into food and fuel for the flames. When this was done, the commotion ceased. Moreover, it is stated that the monster, while it was being borne about (as it is said) by Satan, had told certain persons whom it had by chance encountered, that as long as it remained unburned the people should have no peace. Being burnt, tranquility appeared to be restored to them; but a pestilence, which arose in consequence, carried off the greater portion of them: for never did it so furiously rage elsewhere, though it was at that time general throughout all the borders of England, as shall be more fully explained in its proper place. (William of Newburgh, circa 1200)

Cut Out and Burn the Heart

Here's William of Newburgh again, although we've seen similar reports in maybe a hundred other chronicles, from the Dark Ages up through last Wednesday:

A Christian burial, indeed, he received, though unworthy of it; but it did not much benefit him: for issuing, by the handiwork of Satan, from his grave at night-time, and pursued by a pack of dogs with horrible barkings, he wandered through the courts and around the houses while all men made fast their doors, and did not dare to go abroad on any errand whatever from the beginning of the night until the sunrise, for fear of meeting and being beaten black and blue by this vagrant monster.

Thereupon snatching up a spade of but indifferent sharpness of edge, and hastening to the cemetery, they began to dig; and whilst they were thinking that they would have to dig to a greater depth, they suddenly, before much of the earth had been removed, laid bare the corpse, swollen to an enormous corpulence, with its countenance beyond measure turgid and suffused with blood; while the napkin in which it had been wrapped appeared nearly torn to pieces. The young men, however, spurred on by wrath, feared not, and inflicted a wound upon the senseless carcass, out of which incontinently flowed such a stream of blood, that it might have been taken for a leech filled with the blood of many persons. Then, dragging it beyond the village, they speedily constructed a funeral pile; and upon one of them saying that the pestilential body would not burn unless its heart were torn out, the other laid open its side by repeated blows of the blunted spade, and, thrusting in his hand, dragged out the accursed heart. This being torn piecemeal, and the body now consigned to the flames.

And an account from the magazine *American Anthropologist*, in 1896, demonstrates that this practice is alive and well:

The body of the brother last dead was accordingly exhumed, and "living" blood being found in the heart and in circulation, it was cremated, and the sufferer be-

gan immediately to mend and stood before me a hale, hearty and vigorous man
of fifty years.

Cut Off the Head and Remove the Heart

Maybe not quite as drastic as burning the heart, and an odd thing
about these accounts is that they tend not to mention what happens
to the heart. Fed to wolves, maybe? Thrown in the river? We don't
know. Anyway, decapitation and radical heart-ectomy was the procedure for the shoemaker of Silesia, and also to the revenant in this
account from the abbot of Burton, England, in 1090:

> The very same day in which they were interred they appeared at evening, while
> the sun was still up, carrying on their shoulders the wooden coffins in which they
> had been buried. The whole following night they walked through the paths and
> fields of the village, now in the shape of men carrying wooden coffins on their
> shoulders, now in the likeness of bears or dogs or other animals. They spoke to
> the other peasants, banging on the walls of their houses and shouting, "Move
> quickly, move! Get going! Come!" The villagers became sick and started dying,
> but eventually the bodies of the revenants were exhumed, the heads cut off and
> their hearts removed, which put an end to the spread of the sickness.

A Drive a Stake Through the Head/Mouth/Heart/Stomach

Almost universal. Usually the corpse has to be staked into its coffin,
but sometimes it's enough to stake the revenant/vampire and then
return it to the coffin. The wood of the stake should be hawthorn,
oak, or ash, if possible—although certain groups of Gypsies swear
by the wood of the wild rose tree.

Actually, if you add in the various traditions of needles and
knives and thorns stuck into a corpse's head and feet—while it's
in the coffin—you start to see that your historical vampire hunters
had arrived at a consensus. The other stuff might have worked on

certain occasions, but there's nothing that beats a good old stake to the heart.

So that's what we tried. We used Sam as bait, suckered the zombie girl back to her coffin, and staked her into it. With a silver stake. End of story.

Well, not really.

Other Revenants

Here are samples of some of the other walking dead, mostly taken from Dad's journal:

VRYKOLAKAS

Unconsecrated burial, returns either to murder people in the graveyard or cause problems in the house it left. Sometimes appears as human, other times as a sort of werewolf (although in some versions, the VRYKOLAKAS is destroyed by being dug up and eaten by a wolf). Can drain the life force of the sleeper, similar to succubus/incubus or Mara.

Stories vary widely, often incorporating elements of the poltergeist. Sometimes the VRYKOLAKAS attacks and kills people; other times it plagues their sleep; other times only children die; other times it is only waiting to be dispatched by its surviving family members' fulfillment of a promise. Much overlap between VRYKOLAKAS lore and that of vampires. Not sure if one is a subspecies of the other, or if confusion in the lore has obscured the real differences.

VETALA

Hostile spirits, will animate corpses—their own or others'—to move around. Haunt cemeteries and creation grounds. Will attack in cemeteries; can also drive people mad. Will kill children, possibly to eat, and are known to induce miscarriages. Trapped between the material world and the afterlife, can be dispelled by the performance of funeral rites.

Note: Exorcism will not work on a VETALA. They aren't demons in the sense of the Judeo-Christian ritual. If caught in the right mood, a VETALA might tell you the past and future; for this reason they're much sought-after by sorcerers—mostly resulting in fatal mishaps for those sorcerers, since if caught in the wrong mood, a VETALA is lethal before you know it's there. Best idea is to get on with the funeral rites and send them on their way.

JIANGSHI

"Hopping corpse." Reanimated corpses out of Chinese lore that kill living creatures to feed on SPIRITUS VITAE (qi). Possible that they are restricted to roadways, but I'm working from a story Bobby told me here. Never seen one. Hope I don't.

And there are more. There are *always* more.

WITCHES, FAMILIARS, AND BLACK DOGS

W e've never run into an actual broomstick-riding, pointy-hat-wearing, cauldron-stirring witch, but there are plenty of other kinds of witchcraft, and plenty of other kinds of witches. You've got your *bokor*, your shaman, your *houngan*—the list goes on. What they all have in common is a kind of ritual magic that uses real-world items infused with some kind of magical power. The European witch is usually assumed to be in league with the devil, but in other traditions, witches can be born into their power or make alliances with other supernatural forces.

Often witches are said to have familiars, animals that are bound to them by magical or demonic means. Most often in European witchcraft, the famliar is a cat, but it can also be a toad, an owl, a weasel, or a dog. There are even stories of horses and spiders acting as familiars. In shamanic traditions, the familiar is replaced by the totem animal, which provides some of its qualities to the shaman's—or the tribe's—magic.

Witches who weren't in league with the devil operated in the realm of what's known as folk magic, a kind of gray area between flying a broomstick and traditional practices like midwifery and soothsaying. The local "wise woman" or "wise man" who knew just a little bit more than everyone else about the weather, or herb lore, or medicine was, as likely as not, a practitioner of folk magic. This goes for Europe, but also Africa, South America, and most of the rest of the world. Folk magic is everywhere, and its practitioners are mostly harmless. Some of them, however, put their abilities to darker uses. They might give you the evil eye, in which the concentrated power of the witch's gaze could cause sickness or misfortune. They might hold a grudge against you and cast a spell on your livestock, or your crops, or your children.

When that happened, it was time to fight back. Remedies for magic vary pretty widely across the world, but they also boil down to common elements. Herbs are powerfully protective against many forms of magic and evil intent. (We've put together a list of them at the back of the book, cobbled together from Dad's journals and our own research.) And, as we've mentioned before, there are verbal charms—like "kiss my ass"—that are held to interfere with hostile magic.

There are also more involved methods for protecting your home and loved ones. One of the more interesting ones is the witch bottle, which is a glass or stoneware bottle filled with—well, you don't want to know what they're filled with. Almost always some nails or pins and needles, maybe a little rosemary, maybe a little wine, but add to that all the various possibilities for gross bodily fluids that you can think of, and there you have the traditional witch bottle. The idea is that you put all of this stuff together in the bottle—or have a friendly witch do it—and then you bury the bottle, either under your hearth or in a corner of the house. Then, if a hostile witch comes along and puts some bad magic on you or your house, the magic is trapped in the bottle.

There are two ways to make sure that the magic doesn't get out. In one tradition, you just leave the bottle there. People in England are still discovering witch bottles that have been underground for five hundred years. According to another version, you dug the bottle up every so often and broke it, which would break the magic. Sometimes it would also break the witch.

On this side of the Atlantic, folk magic is pretty well exemplified by what's known as hoodoo. You've heard a million different versions of the old blues song "Got My Mojo Workin'," right? Sure, you have. Well, that "mojo" is a kind of little bag, also known as gris-gris—you'll remember those from our last trip to Lawrence—made of cloth or leather and stuffed with various items that together have a magical effect. Protective mojos might be carried on your person or concealed inside your house. Mojos intended to charm or hex someone else could be placed either in their home or at a crossroads, where the innate magic of the location would do the rest of the work.

You want to draw money? You'll need a Mercury dime, a John the Conqueror root, some sugar, a magnet, and maybe a bit of some kind of oil put together by your local root worker, all in a green flannel bag. Want to drive away evil or break a jinx? That'll take a rat bone, a broken bit of chain, some cinquefoil, and a miniature skull—in a red flannel bag. Maybe you want to put a jinx on someone who stole your woman or owes you money. To get that job done, take some goofer dust, crossroads dirt, spiderwebs, crushed insects, and maybe a powdered snake head. Grind it all together and sprinkle it on the ground in a crossing or wavy pattern where your enemy is sure to step. Spit on it to activate it, and as soon as the intended victim steps on or over it, he'll be afflicted until either you lift the jinx or he figures out some way to get out from under it.

Or do you want to get right down to business and kill someone? For that, you'll need some graveyard dirt, sulfur, some of your enemy's hair or bodily fluid, and nine each of pins, needles, and nails. Put it all in a bottle and bury it under your victim's doorstep, and then sit back and watch the fun. Another method is to put graveyard dirt into the victim's shoe and then drop a pinch of it at every crossroads between his house and the graveyard where you "bought" the dirt.

How does it work? We don't know. It does, though, and we've seen enough to say that with some confidence. We've seen hoodoo necklaces on old women. We've seen haunted dolls animated by the magic of dead witches. We've seen mojo bags buried in the dead of night at crossroads.

And yeah, we've seen black dogs. We keep forgetting to explain the black dogs.

Although witches usually use bats or cats or weasels as familiars, the association of black dogs and unholy practices goes back a long way. An old English legend tells of the Black Shuck, which

appeared from time to time in Anglia and always brought death and misfortune. One of its appearances, in 1577, was chronicled by a local man of the cloth, Abraham Fleming, who wrote an account of the visitation called "A Straunge and Terrible Wunder." The Black Shuck, after wreaking havoc at another area church, burst in on Reverend Fleming's service. Here's how he described the scene:

> This black dog, or the divel in such a likenesse (God hee knoweth al who worketh all,) runing all along down the body of the church with great swiftnesse, and incredible haste, among the people, in a visible fourm and shape, passed between two persons, as they were kneeling uppon their knees, and occupied in prayer as it seemed, wrung the necks of them bothe at one instant clene backward, in somuch that even at a moment where they kneeled, they strangely dyed.

Black dogs were also said to haunt the sites of executions for witchcraft, and various demonic canines populate the annals of European folklore. In most cases, they're either demons taking the form of dogs—that's your classic hellhound that Robert Johnson sang about after he went down to the crossroads—or they're inexplicable supernatural presences. That's the legend Arthur Conan Doyle is borrowing in *The Hound of the Baskervilles*.

It's not just England that associates black dogs with the supernatural, either. In Japan, black dogs were once sacrificed to bring rain. A medieval European superstition held that the first person buried in a churchyard would have to guard all of the souls that followed, so usually a black dog was killed and buried first, and one of the most famous—or notorious, depending on your perspective—magicians of medieval Europe, Cornelius Agrippa, owned a large black dog said to be his familiar. The blood of a black dog was once considered a talisman of good fortune in parts of Asia. And right here in the U.S. of A., there are stories of black dogs that run alongside motorists on what used to be Route 66, sometimes biting through their tires to cause accidents.

These various black dogs could be different kinds of manifestations. Spirits can take all kinds of forms, and shapeshifters might account for some of the sightings. We don't think they can all be explained that way, though. Some of them, at least, are demonic—which means that now it's time to talk about demons.

DEMONS

Those that believe shall cast out demons.

—MARK 16:17

One of our favorite demon anecdotes is from a thirteenth-century French friar, Thomas of Cantimpre. He tells of how a virgin in the town of Nivelles went to church to pray in the middle of the night, after a dead man had been brought into the church. When the devil saw her, "He looked at her with malice, and entering the dead body he moved it at first in the coffin. The virgin therefore crossed herself and bravely shouted to the Devil, 'Lie down! Lie down, you wretch, for you have no power against me!' Suddenly the Devil rose up with the corpse and said, 'Truly, now I will have power against you, and I will revenge myself for the frequent injuries I have suffered at your hands!' When she saw this, she was thoroughly terrified in her heart, so with both hands she seized a staff topped with a cross, and bringing it down on the head of the dead man she knocked him to the ground. Through such faithful daring she put the demon to flight."

We'd have liked to have met that girl.

The thing about demons is that they hate themselves, and so they hate everybody else, too. Ebenezer Sibly, a Renaissance demonologist, gives you both sides of the coin. On the one hand, Sibly notes that demons are who they are because of what they've done. Their physical forms reflect their spiritual state. "As to the shapes and various likenesses of these wicked spirits or devils," Sibly says, "it is generally believed that, according to their different capacities in wickedness, so their shapes are answerable after a magical manner, resembling spiritually some horrid and ugly monsters, as their conspiracies against the power of God were high and monstrous when they fell from heaven."

And the consequences of that fall?

> Their misery is unquestionably great and infinite; but not through the effect of outward flames; for their bodies are capable of piercing through wood and iron, stone, and all terrestrial things. Neither is all the fire or fuel of this world able to torment them; for in a moment they can pierce it through and through.

Their misery, to put it another way, is the misery of someone in hell. Simple as that. The demon that we know only as Meg, whom we threw out a window and then exorcised, is a perfect example of this. She told us, when she came back from hell after the exorcism, a little bit about what it was like. A prison made of flesh and bone and fear is the way we remember her describing it.

Demons come in all shapes and sizes. The one we're really interested in, the one with the yellow eyes who we saw in the hospital where Dean nearly died after the car wreck—the one who killed our mother and Jessica, the one our father traded his life to—we don't have any idea what it looks like. We know it's big-league, some kind of demonic bigwig. Is it Satan? Probably not. It's high enough in the demonic chain of command to have a whole lot of other demons doing its work, though. And it came after our family. That's all we need to want to put it down, and when we say put it down, we mean for keeps. The Yellow-Eyed Demon gets a one-way ticket back to hell, where all of the torments Meg hinted at are its breakfast, lunch, and dinner.

We owe it that much.

In the interest of knowing our enemy, we've done an awful lot of research on demons. A lot of it has piggybacked on the work of earlier demonologists, and some of it has been just a matter of paying attention. For example, you don't need to read John Dee to know that demons stink like sulfur. If you've ever been around one, that's clear enough.

Anyway, here are Dad's notes on some prominent demonology texts and what he thought about each:

A NEW AND COMPLETE ILLUSTRATION OF THE OCCULT SCIENCES (OS)

Written by Ebenezer Sibly. Fourth volume in a series begun 1784 and mostly dedicated to astrology. A disciple of Swedenborg and Mesmer. Makes liberal use of Reginald Scot's DISCOVERIE OF WITCHCRAFT and Agrippa's DE OCCULTA PHILOSOPHIA.

PSEUDOMONARCHIA DAEMONUM (PD)

Written by Johann Weyer, 1563, from a book he calls LIBER OFFICIORUM SPIRITUUM, SEU LIBER DICTUS EMPTO. SALOMONIS, DE PRINCIPIBUS ET REGIBUS DAEMONIORUM (note reference to Solomon here and in Weyer's subtitle: SALOMONS NOTES OF CONJURATION). Weyer a student of Agrippa. The PSEUDOMONARCHIA has much in common with the first book of the LEMEGETON, called GOETIA. A lengthy catalog of demons, with variations on their names, notes on their appearances, and brief instructions on conjuration and abjuration. Translated into English prior to 1584 by Reginald Scot as part of his DISCOVERIE OF WITCHCRAFT. Full of odd notes about how many legions each demon controls, etc. Most of this isn't useful, but the characteristics of individual demons shed some light on the quest.

GOETIA has better diagrams and is more useful for actual conjuration.

THE TESTAMENT OF SOLOMON (TS)

Probably written first to fourth century CE. In Solomon's voice, tells of the building of the Temple and of the binding of numerous demons to perform menial labor. Several of these demons not attested in other sources. The story goes on to tell how Solomon fell in love with a Jebusaean woman (Shunammite?) and desired her for a wife, but was told by the priests of Moloch that he could not have her unless he sacrificed five grasshoppers to Moloch. In a moment of weakness, he did, and fell away from God, becoming "the sport of idols and demons."

One of dozens of texts that characterize Solomon as an arch-magician. Queen of Sheba characterized as a witch, unlike her presentation in the Old Testament. Also interesting that the KORAN refers to the tradition that Solomon built the Temple with the assistance of bound demons: see suras 21, 34, 38.

The PD, in its entry on Gaap, says that Solomon wrote a book of conjurations and "mingled therewithal all the holy names of God."

There are some weird, weird folk remedies for demonic possession. Take this one from a book called *Saxon Leechdoms*, by someone called Cockayne. It's a "spew-drink," which is pretty self-explanatory, and goes like this: "lupin, bishopwort, henbane, cropleek; pound these together, add ale for a liquid, let stand for a night, add fifty libcorns, or cathartic grains, and holy water." It might actually work, is our take. No demon would want to be in the same body with that.

Demons come in all shapes and sizes. There are thousands of named demons in the world's various pantheons—maybe millions if you really do your homework on the Hindus—but there are also categories. Species, maybe, although we've found it never works too well to apply concepts from the natural world to demonology. Here are a few that we've run across and others that we've only heard about. A complete listing would take a lifetime to compile, and we don't even want to think about how long it would take to waste them all.

At the end of the book, we've added a list of the primary demons of Judeo-Christian demonology. For right now, though, here's a quick tour through some examples of what the demon hunter might come up against.

Succubus/ Incubus

Prudish religious types have always cooked up hot, lethal female demons to make everyone think twice about sex. Where we've got the hook man warning us to stay out of Lover's Lane, your medieval Briton or, say, Silesian or Venetian had warnings of the succubus. And if he was a she, the incubus was out there, ready to impregnate her with its demonic seed.

According to some commentators and demonologists, the succubus and incubus were the same demon in two shapes. As a succubus, the demon harvested sperm from its victims, often killing them in the process. Changing shape and becoming male, the demon then passed the sperm along. Since demons couldn't reproduce on their own, they had to be a little ingenious.

Like a lot of other old stories, the succubus one has a noticeable tang of misogyny about it, especially because so many authorities connected succubi to the world's first femme fatale herself: Lilith.

Either Adam's first wife or some kind of proto-feminist demon or both—in some stories she is said to have left Adam because she didn't see any reason why they couldn't swap around their, ahem, standard sexual roles—Lilith has become an archetype of the female demon.

In certain strains of Hebrew myth, incubi and succubi are even called LILIN and LILITH. They are said to be the children of Lilith and to die at a rate of one hundred per day because she would not come back to Adam. They can prey on children—boys until circumcision at eight days, and girls for twenty days—but also attack women by causing infertility and difficult births, even miscarriages. Men become victims of the LILITH by being ridden at night, the seed being used to create more demonic children.

An amulet inscribed with the initials of the three Magi—Caspar, Melchior, and Balthasar—is said to protect children from LILIN and LILITH.

Jinn

An Arabic demon or spirit, created by Allah from smokeless fire. Jinn were created before humans and can be resentful at what they see as the usurpation of the world by humans. They are generally invisible, but they can manifest themselves in a variety of forms and can always see things that are normally visible. Jinns occupy a place in Islam unlike demons in Christianity because the Koran is preached to them as well as to humans. Still, they are often feared. A kind of jinn known as a *marid* had control over water, with all of the power and fickleness that that might imply.

Tengu

This Japanese demon of the mountains is known for misdirecting travelers and possessing the arrogant and prideful, whom the *tengu* will drive mad, or sometimes kill. They possess women in an attempt to seduce holy men (shades of the succubus here, whose favorite target was said in the Middle Ages to be monks). They will desecrate temples.

Abiku

The *abiku* is a West African demon that tempts children away from their homes to eat them. The *abiku* has no stomach and must eat constantly because it can never become full. In other versions, it can dissolve into smoke to get into homes, where it preys on newborns. In general, where demons are concerned, it sucks to be a kid. Other mythologies are chock-full of demons who eat children: the Brazilian Bicho-Papão, Czech Bubak, Egyptian El Nadaha, Iranian *lulu-khorkhore*, Mexican El Cucuy, Quebecois Bonhomme Sept-Heures, Serbian Babaroga, Spanish El Coco, Turkish Dunganga—there are too many to list. Our guess is that there's an archetype here, and that some kind of supernatural monster has spread all over the world indulging its taste for children. We ran into an *abiku* once, preying on a neighborhood of immigrant Nigerians in Queens, New York. The part where it turned to smoke was a bitch, but we got the job done.

Pishacha

These demons from Hindu mythology haunt cremation grounds, and can change shape and turn invisible. Often they possess humans in order to drive them insane. Obviously connected with the revenant *vetala*. Dad had this comment:

> Reminded of the unnamed demon in the TESTA-MENT OF SOLOMON who creeps "beside the men who pass along among the tombs, and in untimely season I assume the form of the dead; and if I catch any one, I at once destroy him with my sword. But if I cannot destroy him, I cause him to be possessed with a demon."

Acheri

Demon that disguises itself as a little girl; from Indian folk tradition. ACHERI are said to inhabit the mountains and murder travelers who are taken in by its helpless guise. A protection against them is to wear a red thread around the neck (this was also said to protect small children against sorcery in some European countries).

The Yellow-Eyed Demon

We know him mostly through his work. He moves into bodies at will. Once he possessed Dad, and we learned something about ourselves there. We could have killed him, but it meant killing Dad, and in the end, it wasn't worth that. All of the stuff that works on other demons doesn't even make him blink. When he was possessing Dad, we doused him in holy water and he didn't even notice. He doesn't leave behind the sulfurous stink that most lesser demons do, either, and ordinary demonic apotropaics like salt and binding sigils don't seem to bother him much. He will respect a summoning if it's perfectly carried out and the summoner has good manners, which is typical of demons. We have a theory that they like to be summoned, since it gets them out of hell, and don't want to ruin their chances at another vacation by dismembering every conju-

ror who comes along. Plus, most of them like to talk. God, do they like to talk. Most of them can be summoned by a standard pentagram doctored with the right ritual candles and so forth, but for the Yellow-Eyed Demon, you need the sigil of Azazel.

The only way to track him is to look for the signs that he's about to strike: increased electrical storms and other freakish weather, temperature fluctuations, livestock diseases—everything but a rain of frogs, if you get the drift. The Yellow-Eyed Son of a Bitch is all Four Horsemen of the Apocalypse rolled into one. The earth itself rebels against his presence—just like it did in the weeks leading up to the fire in our house in Lawrence.

Turns out that the lovely and maniacal Meg (more on her soon) was his daughter, and the other demon we plugged with the Colt was his son. So now there's a family grudge on both sides—but you'll pardon us if we don't feel like we're on equal terms.

There's a war coming, and the Demon is marshaling the forces of the other side. This much we know. And we know that something happened to Sam the night our mother died, and that there are other children like him. How often would you think a child, on the night he turns six months old, would witness the murder of his mother by a demon? Maybe more often than you'd think. We've met five of them now: Max Miller, Andy Gallagher and his twin Ansen Weems, and Ava Wilson. There was another, Scott Carey, but he's not around anymore. Gordon Walker killed him a few days before he tried to get Sam, too. The way Gordon tells it, the six-month children are destined to be part of the Yellow-Eyed Demon's hand-picked elite in his war against humanity.

Life is tough for the six-month kids. Around the time they turn twenty-two, stuff starts happening to them. They develop abilities. ESP is a word for it, but it varies with the individual. Andy's got some serious mind-control mojo, and so did Ansen. Scott Carey apparently was pyrokinetic, Max Miller telekinetic. And Sam Winchester has premonitions.

You'll notice we used the past tense there a couple of times. Ansen Weems and Max Miller are dead, victims of their own powers running away with them. And like we said, Gordon Walker got Scott. We managed to save Andy Gallagher.

Exactly what the Demon's plan is, we don't know. And we're hoping never to find out, because that would mean we'd tracked that son of a bitch down and sent him back to hell for good.

Lesser Demons We Have Known

The first demon we ran into after reuniting Winchester and Sons had a thing for crashing airplanes, which is something they like to do. Haunt ships and planes, even cars. Probably they used to haunt chariots and triremes, too. Anyway, before we figured out what it was, we got a little refresher course in EVP, or electronic voice phenomena. That's when things get recorded on tape that nobody in the room actually said. And it sure was happening here, because on the cockpit voice recorder of this most recent crashed plane, Britannia flight 2485, a voice was clearly saying, "No survivors . . . no survivors . . ."

Except there *were* survivors of this particular crash, which occurred after one of the passengers ripped open the emergency door in midflight, which is impossible for a normal human being to do. Seven survivors, one of whom, from his new residence in a mental hospital, said that the guy who opened the door had black eyes.

A picture was starting to emerge here, and it was confirmed after we talked our way into the NTSB warehouse storing the wreckage and found sulfur all over the door handle.

Demon.

And, like most problems with demons, this one got worse and more complicated before it got better. We figured out that this demon had haunted flights before and brought them all down forty minutes after takeoff. Now it was after the survivors of flight 2485.

Which meant we had to figure out which one of them it was going to go after, and that turned out to be a stewardess. To make a long story short, we performed a full-on exorcism in midair while the demon was trying to crash the plane with us in it.

The *Rituale Romanum*, man. Don't leave home without it. Guaranteed to first make a demon manifest, and then blow it back to hell. Here it is, the whole shebang, in the original Latin. Usually you only need the first round of the three, but you should memorize the whole thing, because there is literally nothing worse than not being able to exorcise a demon when you really, really need to.

OREMUS ORATIO

Deus, et Pater Domini nostri Jesu Christi, invoco nomen sanctum tuum, et clementiam tuam supplex exposco: ut adversus hunc, et omnem immundum spiritum, qui vexat hoc plasma tuum. Mihi auxilium praestare igneris. Per eumdem Dominum. Amen.

EXORCISMUS

Exorcizo te, immundissime spiritus, omnis incursio adversarii, omne phantasma, omnis legio, in nomine Domini nostri Jesu Christi eradicare, et effugare ab hoc plasmate Dei. Ipse tibi imperat, qui te de supernis caelorum in inferiora terrae demergi praecepit. Ipse tibi imperat, qui mari, ventis, et tempestatibus imperavit. Audi ergo, et time, satana, inimice fidei, hostis generis humani, mortis adductor, vitae raptor, justitiae declinator, malorum radix, fomes vitiorum, seductor hominum, proditor gentium, incitator invidiae, origo avaritiae, causa discordiae, excitator dolorum: quid stas, et resistis, cum scias. Christum Dominum vias tuas perdere? Illum metue, qui in isaac immolatus est, in joseph venumdatus, in agno occisus, in homine crucifixus, deinde inferni triumphator fuit. Sequentes cruces fiant in fronte obsessi. Recede ergo in nomine Patris et Filii, et Spiritus Sancti: da locum Spiritui Sancto, per hoc signum sanctae Crucis Jesu Christi Domini nostri: Qui cum Patre et eodem Spiritu Sancto vivit et regnat Deus, per omnia saecula saeculorum. Amen.

OREMUS   ORATIO

Deus, conditor et defensor generis humani, qui hominem ad imaginem tuam formasti: respice super hunc famulum tuum (N), qui dolis immundi spiritus appetitur, quem vetus adversarius, antiquus hostis terrae, formidinis horrore circumvolat, et sensum mentis humanae stupore defigit, terrore conturbat, et metu trepidi timoris exagitat. Repelle, Domine, virtutem diaboli, fallacesque ejus insidias amove: procul impius tentator aufugiat. sit nominis tui signo (in fronte) famulus tuus munitus et in animo tutus et corpore (Tres cruces sequentes fiant in pectore daemoniaci). Tu pectoris hujus interna custodias. Tu viscera regas. Tu cor confirmes. In anima adversatricis potestatis tentamenta evanescant. Da, Domine, ad hanc invocationem sanctissimi nominis tui gratiam, ut, qui hucusque terrebat, territus aufugiat, et victus abscedat, tibique possit hic famulus tuus et corde firmatus et mente sincerus, debitum praebere famulatum. Per Dominum. Amen.

EXORCISMUS

Adjuro te, serpens antique, per judicem vivorum et mortuorum, per factorem tuum, per factorem mundi, per eum, qui habet potestatem mittendi te in gehennam, ut ab hoc famulo Dei (N), qui ad Ecclesiae sinum recurrit, cum metu, et exercitu furoris tui festinus discedas. Adjuro te iterum (in fronte) non mea infirmitate, sed virtute Spiritus Sancti, ut exeas ab hoc famulo Dei (N), quem omnipotens Deus ad imaginem suam fecit. Cede igitur, cede non mihi, sed ministro Christi. Illius enim te urget potestas, qui te Cruci suae subjugavit. Illius brachium contremisce, qui devictis gemitibus inferni, animas ad lucem perduxit. sit tibi terror corpus hominis (in pectore), sit tibi formido imago Dei (in fronte). Non resistas, nec moreris discedere ab homine isto, quoniam complacuit Christo in homine habitare. Et ne contemnendum putes, dum me peccatorem nimis esse cognoscis. Imperat tibi Deus. Imperat tibi majestas Christi imperat tibi Deus Pater, imperat tibi Deus Filius, imperat tibi Deus Spiritus Sanctus. Imperat tibi

Crossroads demons.

The Yellow-Eyed Demon.

Lesser demons: 3 of the 7 deadly sins (top) and Meg (above), the YED's daughter.

Vampires: 'good' (top; captured by Walker), bad (above), and confused (opposite top).

A reaper.

Bobby attempts to exorcise 'Meg' from Sam's body.

Possessed Sam under the Devil's Trap.

Bobby destroys the brand binding 'Meg' to Sam's body.

Sam draws a powerful protection pentagram, and reveals his anti-possession tattoo.

sacramentum crucis. Imperat tibi fides sanctorum Apostolorum Petri et Pauli, et ceterorum Sanctorum. Imperat tibi Martyrum sanguis. Imperat tibi continentia Confessorum. Imperat tibi pia sanctorum et sanctarum omnium intercessio. Imperat tibi christianae fidei mysteriorum virtus. Exi ergo, transgressor. Exi, seductor, plene omni dolo et fallacia, virtutis inimice, innocentium persecutor. Da locum, dirissime, da locum, impiissime, da locum Christo, in quo nihil invenisti de operibus tuis: qui te spoliavit, qui regnum tuum destruxit, qui te victum ligavit, et vasa tua diripuit: qui te projecit in tenebras exteriores, ubi tibi cum ministris tuis erit praeparatus interitus. Sed quid truculente reniteris? Quid temerarie detrectas? Reus es omnipotenti Deo, cujus statuta transgressus es. Reus es Filio ejus Jesu Christo Domino nostro, quem tentare ausus es, et crucifigere praesumpsisti. Reus es humano generi, cui tuis persuasionibus mortis venenum propinasti.

Adjuro ergo te, draco nequissime, in nomine Agni immaculati, qui ambulavit super aspidem et basiliscum, qui conculcavit leonem et draconem, ut discedas ab hoc homine (fiat signum crucis in fronte), discedas ab Ecclesia Dei (fiat signum crucis super circumstantes): contremisce, et effuge, invocato nomine Domini illius, quem inferi tremunt: cui Virtutes caelorum, et Potestates, et Dominationes subjectae sunt: quem Cherubim et seraphim indefessis vocibus laudant, dicentes: Sanctus, sanctus, sanctus Dominus Deus sabaoth. Imperat tibi Verbum caro factum. Imperat tibi natus ex Virgine. Imperat tibi Jesus Nazarenus, qui te, cum discipulos ejus contemneres, elisum atque prostratum exire praecepit ab homine: quo praesente, cum te ab homine separasset, nec porcorum gregem ingredi praesumebas. Recede ergo nunc adjuratus in nomine ejus ab homine, quem ipse plasmavit. Durum est tibi velle resistere. Durum est tibi contra stimulum calcitrare. Quia quanto tardius exis, tanto magis tibi supplicium crescit, quia non homines contemnis, sed illum, qui dominatur vivorum et mortuorum, qui venturus est judicare vivos et mortuos, et saeculum per ignem. Amen.

OREMUS   ORATIO

Deus caeli, Deus terrae, Deus Angelorum, Deus Archangelorum, Deus Prophetarum, Deus Apostolorum, Deus Martyrum, Deus Virginum, Deus, qui potestatem habes donare vitam post mortem, requiem post laborem: quia non est alius Deus praeter te, nec esse poterit verus, nisi tu, Creator caeli et terrae, qui verus Rex es, et cujus regni non erit finis; humiliter majestati gloriae tuae supplico, ut hunc famulum tuum de immundis spiritibus liberare digneris. Per Christum Dominum Nostrum. Amen.

EXORCISMUS

Adjuro ergo te, omnis immundissime spiritus, omne phantasma, omnis incursio satanae, in nomine Jesu Christi Nazareni, qui post lavacrum Joannis in desirtum ductus est, et te in tuis sedibus vicit: ut, quem ille de limo terrae ad honorem gloriae suae formavit, tu desinas impugnare: et in homine miserabili non humanam fragilitatem, sed imaginem omnipotentis Dei contremiscas. Cede ergo Deo qui te, et malitiam tuam in Pharaone, et in exercitu ejus per Moysen servum suum in abyssum demersit. Cede Deo qui te per fidelissimum servum suum

David de rege Saule spiritualibus canticis pulsum fugavit. Cede Deo qui te in Juda Iscariote proditore damnavit. Ille enim te divinis verberibus tangit, in cujus conspectu cum tuis legionibus tremens et clamans dixisti: Quid nobis et tibi, Jesu, Fili Dei altissimi? Venisti huc ante tempus torquere nos? Ille te perpetuis flammis urget, qui in fine temporum dicturus est impiis: Discedite a me, maledicti, in ignem aeternum, qui paratus est diabolo et angelis ejus. Tibi enim, impie, et angelis tuis vermes erunt, qui numquam morientur. Tibi, et angelis tuis inexstinguibile praeparatur incendium: quia tu es princeps maledicti homicidii, tu auctor incestus, tu sacrilegorum caput, tu actionum pessimarum magister, tu haereticorum doctor, tu totius obscoenitatis inventor. Exi ergo, impie, exi, scelerate, exi cum omni fallacia tua: quia hominem templum suum esse voluit Deus. Sed quid diutius moraris hic? Da honorem Deo Patri omnipotenti, cui omne genu flectitur. Da locum Domino Jesu Christo, qui pro homine sanguinem suum sacratissimum fudit. Da locum Spiritui Sancto, qui per beatum Apostolum suum Petrum te manifeste stravit in Simone mago; qui fallaciam tuam in Anania et Saphira condemnavit; qui te in Herode rege honorem Deo non dante percussit; qui te in mago Elyma per Apostolum suum Paulum caecitatis caligine perdidit, et per eumden de Pythonissa verbo imperans exire praecepit. Discede ergo nunc, discede, seductor. Tibi eremus sedes est. Tibi habitatio serpens est: humiliare, et prosternere. Jam non est differendi tempus. Ecce enim dominator Dominus proximat cito, et ignis ardebit ante ipsum, et praecedet, et inflammabit in circuitu inimicos ejus. Si enim hominem fefelleris, Deum non poteris ir-

The next time we had to use the *Rituale* was on a pretty little thing named Meg, who apart from being blond and cute was possessed by a seriously sadistic demon of above-average toughness. She was enough of a badass to conjure and control daevas, which puts her definitely in the major leagues. What's a daeva, you ask? Well. There are demons, and then there are *demons*. Daevas are real assassins. No black-eyed, fooling-around possession for them. You only see their shadows, and by the time you see that, you're already dead. They're Zoroastrian and mean enough and scary enough that we get our word "devil" from them.

And like we said, Meg had them on a leash.

What you need in order to do this is a serious black altar, of the kind that we've only seen twice, the kind that would make Anton LaVey wake up screaming in the night. This kind of black altar is soaked in human blood, made partly of bones, with dried human hearts in an offertory bowl and its altar-cloth tassels made from human hair. With that kind of altar, you can do some powerful necromancy, and Meg sure had the knowhow.

So she had the daevas, and she wasn't afraid to use them.

We found out about Meg—who Sam had run into a couple of months before, pretending she was just on a bus trip across the country—because of an unsolved murder in Chicago in which the victim, Meredith McDonnell, was torn apart and her heart removed. Our kind of thing. Werewolf, we were thinking. Then we talked our way into the scene, where we found that the victim's blood had been carefully dripped around the floor to form symbols:

Later that night, we asked around Meredith's workplace, the Firetop Bar, and right as we're reading a newspaper article about another savage murder much like that of Meredith McDonnell, who should walk in but Meg.

What a coincidence. You run into a girl in a bus stop in Indiana; she's on her way to California. Months later she's in Chicago, in the same bar you just walked into. Small world.

Maybe even a little *too* coincidental, we were sort of half-heartedly thinking, but she was hot, and Sam was lonely, and Dean was looking out for his little brother—and the end result was that when Sam stealthily followed his crush out that night, she just so happened to wander into a warehouse in which there was this real gruesome black altar with two human hearts on it. You know, right after two locals had been killed and their hearts removed. And on the altar was the same sign that was on Meredith McDonnell's floor.

A daeva sigil.

We put our heads together, and at about the same time we find out that both of the murder victims were natives of... Lawrence, Kansas.

That was a little too much coincidence for either of us. It was time to have a little chat with Meg.

Which didn't go the way we'd planned, actually, because she'd been playing us the whole time. She knew we were coming, and she sicced the daevas on us, and before we knew what hit us, we were tied up in chairs, bait for Dad. Who was Meg's *real* target.

Now, we might be easily turned into idiots when there are pretty girls around, but we're at our best when tied to chairs with bloodthirsty demons about to dismember us. Dean accidentally made a noise while trying to get free, so Meg came over to get things under control—only to find that Sam had slipped loose. Over went the black altar, and the daevas went over Meg, and Meg went out the window from seven stories up.

Later that night, we had a family reunion. First time all three of us had been together since Sam decided to go to college. And then the daevas crashed the party, and it was time to get the hell out of Chicago.

We thought we were done with her, but it turned out we didn't know Meg very well. The next time we ran into her was after she called to tell us that she'd killed two of Dad's oldest friends, Pastor Jim Murphy and Caleb, whose last name we don't think even Dad ever knew. Hunter culture is like that. Meg threatened to keep on offing his friends unless he brought her the Colt, and he agreed—though of course, being Dad, he brought a fake and left the real one with us, because the Demon was supposed to appear in Salvation, Iowa, that night. That's Dad, taking a fake gun to a nest of demons to make sure we got our shot at the Big Kahuna.

It almost worked—but close doesn't count in demon hunting. When we saw Meg face-to-face, out at Bobby Singer's, she had Dad held hostage in a warehouse in Jefferson City, Missouri. We didn't know this, though; we needed to get it out of her. Figuring that she'd never tell us, we decided to exorcise her and hope that her human host would know. We had no idea whether the plan would work, since at that point neither of us had ever been possessed, and from what we knew of the lore, there was no way to predict whether the host would remember anything that happened during the possession.

Plus there was the complication that the last time we'd seen Meg, we'd thrown her out a window, and another demon we'll call Tom—who turned out to be her brother—had shot her to see if the Colt was real, so her human body was definitely on demonic life support.

To trap a demon as strong as Meg, you need more than your typical pentagram. You need something like the protective circle from the *Clavicula Solomonis,* or *Key of Solomon.* It looks a little something like this:

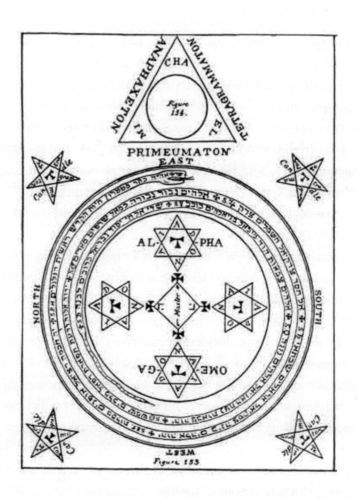

Once you've got that, and your *Rituale Romanum* handy, you're ready to do some business with your demon. Which we did, exorcising Meg and sending her back to hell. What was left behind was this dying girl, agonized and grateful to us because we'd let her die after everything she'd felt her possessed body doing. Nobody should ever have to feel that. And we were partly responsible for it. We let her die.

And then we headed off to Jefferson City to get Dad back.

Meg had told us the Demon was there and that he would want the Colt. She was right on both counts, as we found out after we stormed in there, wasted a couple of demons, and got the hell out with Dad. Two hours later, out in the middle of nowhere, we found out that the Demon had played his best joke yet. He was in Dad, and he was going to kill us, slowly, and make us watch each other's deaths. But the Demon hadn't counted on Dad, who was, hands down, the toughest SOB we ever knew. Dad got hold of his own body long enough for Sam to grab the Colt, and Sam plugged him in the leg. Knocked him down, hard, with Samuel Colt's magic burning through him and Dad now strong enough—just barely—to hold the Demon inside him so we could kill it.

We had it. We had it there, trapped in our father, and we could have ended the whole thing right then. Could have made the whole crusade of our lives worthwhile.

Except, you know, we couldn't. Because he was in our *father*.

So that's the story about how we let the Demon, who's planning a war against all that is good in humanity, get away. Because some things are more important. Family is more important.

And that wasn't the last we heard of Meg, either—or Gordon Walker. Seems Gordon tickled some information out of a demon and found out about the six-month children, and the demon let him know that Sam was one of them. So, Gordon being Gordon, he decided that a preemptive strike was the best course. Meaning he decided he'd kill all of the six-month children before they got a chance to be drafted into the Demon's army. He killed Scott Carey and then took a shot at Sam before we turned the tables on him and arranged for a local police department to find him armed to the teeth in the immediate vicinity of some recently deceased people.

From one perspective, that's a dirty trick. From another, it's a means of survival. And the truth is, we felt bad about it, except when we remembered that Gordon had tried to kill Sam. We thought that when we turned Gordon Walker over to the police, in a really compromising situation, that we had done about the worst thing one hunter could do to another. That is, until Sam got possessed by a demon and killed Steve Wandel.

We'd never met Steve, but we knew he was a hunter. He hung around Harvelle's, and we'd probably seen him in passing. Probably he had known Dad, before Dad traded his own life—and the Colt— to save Dean in the aftermath of the car accident. But once Steve was dead, we had a problem. Word was already out on the hunter grapevine that something wasn't quite right with the Winchesters, and if it ever got out that Sam had killed Steve Wandel—even if it was really a demon that had done it—we'd have been exiled. *If* we managed to stay alive.

The first thing we had to do, though, was an exorcism on Sam. After a little run-in involving Jo Harvelle and Dean, Sam headed for

his next target, and that's where he made his first mistake. The demon possessing him got a little overeager and went after Bobby Singer. Bobby, who knows his ass from a hole in the ground, knew right away that something was wrong with Sam. He spiked Sam's beer with holy water and, while Sam was recovering, tied him up under a Devil's Trap. What can we say; Bobby's got style.

Anyway, this is when things got even more complicated.

When Bobby tried to exorcise the demon possessing Sam, we found out that the demons had started to work on ways to counter the binding rituals. In this case, the demon was Meg, who had a personal grudge against us for the way we treated her the year before, and she had managed to figure out how to break the Devil's Trap.

Spiritus immundi, ungularum suarum emittite paulatim iram. Domina, persona carnis ossisque, toti mundi, trepidationais pennarum, tu appellatus vir, veritas et mensura. In murum somni pii, spiritus immundi, ungularum suarum emittite paulatim iram.

Near as we can figure, this is a Black Mass–style inversion of a *spiritus mundi*. The bad guys are always trying to keep up with us. So far we've generally managed to stay just a little ahead. This time, though, there was a binding involved. Sometimes, if it's worried about running afoul of an exorcist, a demon will bind itself inside a body. Usually the way to do this is through a brand or a scar, which has to be destroyed before the demon can be exorcised. This time, the demon got the jump on us by binding itself into Sam by burning a symbol onto his arm. And since the demon was Meg, who as we've mentioned before is pretty tough, and who was not in the least bit happy about having been sent back to hell, things were looking bleak for the Winchester boys...

Until Bobby laid a hot fireplace poker on the binding symbol and burned it into oblivion.

Then, because the exorcism had already happened, Meg had to go. We only wish we'd finished the whole thing, so we could have watched her melt back into the hell she'd come from. The hell she'd brought with her, both for Sam and for Steve Wandel.

Reaper

The other time we saw a black altar was when the wife of a traveling preacher was using it to bind a reaper. That's some serious necromancy, too, and about the last place in the world we expected to find it was behind the tent at a religious revival. This binding spell involved a vial of human blood built into a Coptic cross, and the whole black altar in the basement shtick. Once the vial of blood broke, the reaper came for the preacher's wife, restoring the balance she'd upset when she bound it. Necromancy is about creating that kind of imbalance, and if whatever is bound by necromancy gets free, the first thing it does is take the necromancer's life as part of the restoration of that balance. In this case, the reaper took the preacher's wife and that was that. Reapers aren't exactly demons—near as we can tell, they don't take sides in the whole good-versus-evil thing—they're just death given form, and they operate as what's called a psychopomp. Dad had a bit about the psychopomp in his journal:

> Psychopomp. Term for god or entity responsible for guiding souls to the afterlife. In Greece, Hermes. In Norse myth, the Valkyries. In Egypt, Anubis. Voodoo traditions, going back to their African roots, offer Ghede. Irish, Ankou. In most shamanic traditions, the shaman is a sort of psychopomp both at the beginning of life and at the end. He or she was present at birth to usher the child into the world, and present at death to see the soul on its journey. Medieval legends of the sickle-bearing Grim Reaper perhaps connected to practice in some parts of Europe whereby the dead were stabbed or buried with sickles. The real reapers are purely psychic entities, with power over time and perception. They can change the way a human sees his surroundings and change their own appearance, usually to ease the transition from life into death. The reaper's true form is hard to pin down, but most accounts suggest that the natural way for a living person to see a reaper is as a wraith-like figure wearing tattered winding sheets or burial cloth.

We'll just add that we can attest to the fact that the reaper is a powerful illusionist. Dean, near death after the encounter with the Demon and the car accident that followed, had a long conversation with a reaper who looked kind of like Meg Tilly back when Meg Tilly was hot.

We even read somewhere that Peter Pan is a kind of psycho-pomp figure, because in the book it says that when children die he leads them part of the way so they won't be afraid. Jeez, way to ruin a good kid's story.

Goofer Dust

Hoodoo tradition has also given us one of the best anti-witchcraft charms we've ever heard of. Recorded throughout African-American populations in the South, it goes like this: if you see a witch, all you have to do to keep from being hexed is repeat "kiss my ass" under your breath as long as the witch is there. We do this on general principle, pretty much 24/7, just in case there's a witch around.

APPENDIX A
Herbs, Oils, and Hoodoo Hands

Here's a list, or a sort of glossary, of various sacred herbs and other materials used in magical traditions from the ancient Egyptian to the medieval European to the folk-magic practitioners of today. Be warned: this stuff works.

AGRIMONY: Powerful defensive herb that not only can prevent hexes and banish evil spirits, but often will reverse the effects of a spell onto the caster. In addition, agrimony can be used in a potion to induce a deep sleep almost indistinguishable from death.

ALFALFA: Traditionally used in combination with other herbs to bring good fortune. Not extremely powerful on its own, but very useful when added to charms against poverty or bad luck. In Celtic traditions, alfalfa is often burned and the ashes scattered around the outside of a house as protection against poverty and hunger.

ALLSPICE: Like alfalfa, more of a catalyst than an individual power. It's often used as an element of charms involving money and luck. Allspice has an interesting association with creativity and in some traditions is used to spark a brainstorm or artistic inspiration.

AMARANTH: Known for its protective abilities and for use in calling spirits. A whole amaranth plant, uprooted under a full moon and then worn under the shirt, is a powerful protection against physical attacks. The dried flowers are useful in calling the dead.

ANGELICA: Also known as "archangel," angelica root is very powerful in protective functions. Sprinkled in the four corners of a house, it protects against evil, and it is a powerful talisman when carried on the person. Used at the beginning and ending of rituals, it has a strong blessing effect. Also associated with good luck, particularly in certain native American traditions, where it was used to bring fortune in gambling. Smoking the leaves can cause visions.

ANISE: Raises vibrations to the highest possible psychic level. Good for bringing about changes in attitude (refocusing), for astral travel, dreams, crystal gazing, and meditation. In a pillow, it is said to keep away nightmares. For any type of clairvoyance or divination or mental exercises. Anisette (liquor) is used during voodoo initiations to anoint the head.

ANOINTING OIL: The biblical tradition of anointing with oil stems from a specific oil mentioned in Exodus 30, which was composed of cinnamon, calamus, cassia, and myrrh, infused in olive oil. This oil is an important element in the performance of certain protective rituals.

ASAFETIDA: Also known as devil's dung or stinking gum for its odor, asafetida is a very powerful protectant. When burned, it will drive away evil and dispel spirits. It can be used in various rituals of exorcism. It is also said to attract wolves.

BALM OF GILEAD: Also known as balsam of Mecca. A resinous gum extracted from the balsam poplar tree. Known for its protective and healing properties since biblical times.

BARBERRY: A dangerous herb, more suited to dark magic than positive uses. When sprinkled around a house, will provoke argument and bitterness. This effect can be reversed if barberry is combined with bay leaves and vetivert, but this forces the herb to operate against its nature and is a tricky undertaking.

BASIL: Used in a wide variety of rituals and sachets to purify, protect, and increase harmony and well-being. If sprinkled over a sleeping lover, it will ensure both fidelity and sexual interest. Ubiquitous in spells of love and prosperity. Basil can be burned as incense in certain exorcism rituals and when sprinkled on the floor provides some protection against the physical presence of evil.

BAY: The visions of the Delphic oracle are said to have been the product of chewing bay leaves. They also will induce visions when burned and when placed under the pillow can bring prophetic dreams. In potions, bay leaves can bring a kind of clairvoyance, and when the leaves are kept on the person, they will protect against evil—although in some traditions this is reversed, and the bay's power is said to be in its use for hexing others.

BAYBERRY: Traditionally used in the manufacture of candles, bayberry works as a powerful catalyst for the magical properties of other herbs—usually in a negative direction. Can be used to cause depression and to force the collection of debts. Also can be used to attract a male lover, though the bayberry's magical complexion makes the wisdom of such a romance questionable.

BELLADONNA: Apart from its use in optometry to dilate pupils, belladonna has a number of magical properties. It is extremely dangerous to use, being toxic in any but the tiniest amounts. Carefully employed, however, it can be used to facilitate bilocation and astral projection, as well as visionary states. Belladonna is often used in funeral rituals to ease the passage of the soul between worlds. It is also known as nightshade, and some folklore suggests that application of belladonna can prevent someone bitten by a werewolf from becoming one.

BENZOIN: Another herb whose primary use is as an intensifier. Particularly noted for its combination with cinnamon; when burned together, these herbs bring material success. Very dangerous if used to increase the power of a hex or negative spell. Mixed and burned with dittany of Crete, sandalwood, and vanilla, benzoin forms a powerful aid to astral projection.

BERGAMOT: The leaves, if rubbed on money, will ensure wise spending. If placed in the wallet, they are said to attract money. Bergamot is also reputed to enhance intuition and can be used in various combinations to induce prophetic dreams.

BETONY: Druidic rituals employed betony in several capacities. At midsummer, it was added to bonfires, and those who jumped through the smoke would be purified of malevolent influences. Dried and placed inside a pillow, it ensures restful sleep and wards off nightmares.

BINDWEED: Useful in both protective and aggressive magic, bindweed overwhelms the intentions of its target. Depending on the other herbs in the charm, it can be employed to control another person or simply thwart his intentions. Not to be taken internally, since it is a powerful laxative and purgative.

BISTORT: When used in conjunction with juniper and allspice, bistort will draw money. It is also used to help couples conceive a child.

BLACKBERRY: Sacred to a number of pagan deities, the blackberry is a powerful protective plant. It is often used as part of a wreath, in combination with ivy and rowan, which when placed at the door will ward off evil. A blackberry bramble that grows in a natural arch is said to be both a gateway to the fairy realm and a strong healing location. If crawled through both backward and forward, the arch will cure numerous bodily ailments.

BLACK SNAKEROOT: When used by a man, black snakeroot can be a powerful charm to create or destroy love. If burned with objects related to an individual, the root exerts a powerful repelling influence on that person; its opposite function is to compel love when burned with Adam and Eve root.

BLUEBERRY: Whether eaten or used as a charm or sachet, blueberry is an extremely potent protection against treachery and deception. Eating blueberries increases an individual's ability to resist psychic influence or assault. Placed near the door of a household, it will keep unwanted visitors away.

BUCHU LEAVES: Native to southern Africa, buchu has been incorporated into various New World divination rituals. Burned with frankincense, buchu can bring prophetic dreams; taken as an infusion it can strengthen powers of clairvoyance.

BURDOCK: In the Middle Ages, knights often rode into battle with a sprig of burdock, which was said to protect and promote healing, particularly of the feet. A charm of burdock root, gathered under a waning moon and strung around the neck, will ward away evil influences.

CACAO: Considered food of the gods by the Aztecs and often used in potions and charms to gain love or throw off malign influences. It is also used to quiet angry or restless spirits and is a standard element of Latin American séances.

CALAMUS: Often used as a binding element in charms or spells, calamus can also be used by itself to control an individual. Grown in a garden, it will bring luck to the gardener and enhance the yield of the plants close to it.

CALENDULA: More familiarly known as the marigold, calendula is used in a variety of ways. In certain rituals, it is said to give knowledge of the language of birds. Burned as incense, the petals consecrate objects intended for use in divinatory rituals. Another use of the marigold is in rituals to attain a clairvoyant state or to communicate with supernatural beings.

CAMPHOR: Often used as part of cleansing rituals, camphor is also frequently used in charms to end unwanted romantic entanglements or lessen desire.

CARAWAY: Said to be a potent protective herb, especially against Lilith and malign spirits of a sexual nature. Also frequently used in spells and charms designed to beguile a lover. A parallel tradition holds that any object—for example, a wallet or purse—containing caraway seeds cannot be stolen.

CARDAMOM: Although it is sometimes said to have powerful properties of its own where love and lust are concerned, cardamom is most often used to catalyze the effect of other herbs in sexual or love spells.

CAROB: The pods of this plant are often used as part of charms to attract wealth, but carob's more esoteric uses include burning as incense to repel poltergeists or—when used by a witch—to attract a familiar.

CATNIP: Once chewed by warriors before battle to increase their ferocity, catnip is used to aid in the creation of the bond between a witch and a cat familiar and is generally known to increase the intensity of psychic abilities. Also, the leaves can be dried and burned as part of love/sex rituals.

CAYENNE: One of the more powerful catalysts in the herbal repertoire, especially as part of spells intended to control, cayenne is equally useful in creating or breaking hexes. It is also a strong ingredient in counterspells and can reverse the effects of a negative spell on the caster.

CEDAR: The smoke of the cedar is a common ingredient in psychic rituals and is also used to prevent nightmares.

CHAMOMILE: Traditionally used to protect from the evil eye or to break curses, chamomile is a gentle yet powerful agent in various love and prosperity rituals. Often it is used to prepare the mind and body for magic, due to its calming and centering properties.

CINNAMON: A powerful part of spells designed for psychic power or control, cinnamon is especially protective when burned in a mixture of sandalwood, frankincense, and myrrh. It is a common ingredient in spells or charms intended to capture male love or lust.

CLOVE: Often used to add force to a hex, cloves are powerful catalysts in spells of exorcism and purification. Also they are worn or carried to offer protection from evil spirits and in many traditions are strung over cribs to protect infants.

CLOVER: Generally used as a ward against evil and bad fortune, clover is also an important element in rituals of clairvoyance. Holding a four-leaf clover conveys the power to see fairies and detect the presence of spirits.

COMFREY LEAF: An important part of spells to protect travelers, comfrey leaf is also incorporated into rituals of spiritual projection.

CUBEB: A form of pepper native to Indonesia, cubeb was included in medieval rituals to repel demons, particularly the incubus. This antisexual property is reversed in hoodoo practice, which often uses the berries as part of love magic.

CUMIN: Mixed with salt, cumin is part of a common household charm to repel evil and bad luck. It is also used as a binding influence in spells that require a lighter touch rather than pure magical force.

DAMIANA: Particularly in Latin American traditions that stem from Mayan and Aztec lore, damiana is used as an aphrodisiac and component in sex magic. It is also an important part of rituals to bring about visionary states.

DANDELION: Dried and used as tea, the roots and leaves of the dandelion call spirits and enhance psychic abilities. In Celtic paganism, Samhain rituals made use of dandelion for divination.

DEVIL'S BIT: Often substituted for low John, or galangal, in hoodoo magic, devil's bit adds compulsive and controlling power to whatever charm it is made part of, whether involving exorcism, love, or protection.

ECHINACEA: Apart from its healing and protective properties, echinacea was used in various Native American traditions as an offering to spirits, who would then strengthen the shaman's magic.

ELDER: The leaves of the elder, gathered at the right time and place, prevent witches from entering a house. It is used in divination, but the tree's magic is ambivalent, since it is associated with witchcraft and walking under an elder can bring the attention of malign forces.

ELECAMPANE: Named *inula* by the Greeks because of their belief that Helen of Troy carried a bunch of it away to Phrygia at her abduction by Paris, elecampane is a powerful element in love charms and also improves the potency of scrying rituals.

FENNEL: Sacred in both the Anglo-Saxon and kabbalistic traditions, fennel is part of meditative rituals and counterspells to remove hexes. In the Middle Ages, fennel was combined with St. John's wort in a midsummer ritual to prevent witchcraft and repel evil spirits. Somewhat unpredictable, fennel can prevent possession but also twist the function of other herbs and magical processes.

FENUGREEK: The Egyptians buried fenugreek in the tombs of certain pharaohs, including Tutankhamen. It is associated with luck and success.

FIG: Sacred to Dionysus and Juno, among others, the fig was also used in rituals around the Celtic holiday Beltane. Also it is an important part of divination rituals in virtually every culture where it is known.

FIVE FINGER GRASS: Also known as cinquefoil, this herb is useful in protecting against hexes, but when mixed with soot its influence reverses, and it becomes a potent hexing agent itself.

FRANKINCENSE: Used as a divinatory offering across times and cultures, frankincense is part of numerous exorcism and protection rituals as well. Often it provides a stable base around which other elements are combined into an incense. When burned in conjunction with myrrh—the feminine counterpart to its masculine association—frankincense provides a balancing influence on charms and rituals.

GALANGAL: Also known as low John, this root is most useful in creating change where subtle and indirect means will be more successful than direct action. A tricky and somewhat devious herb, it is, when used properly, a powerful breaker of spells and protector of health. As part of hoodoo practice, it will bring money if placed in a leather sachet with silver.

GALBANUM OIL: The sixteenth-century grimoire *Liber Juratus* refers to this oil, a simple infusion of galbanum resin. According to the *Juratus*, it is used in rituals aiming to contact both angels and spirits.

GARLIC: Long before it was used to ward off vampires, garlic was part of Greek ritual, being placed on stone cairns at crossroads as a sacrifice to Hecate. An Islamic legend states that garlic first grew out of the prints of Satan's left foot as he left the Garden of Eden. (Onions grew from the right.) Soldiers from Roman times through the medieval period ate garlic before battle to protect them and give them courage. Garlic hung over the door of a home not only wards away evil but prevents an envious person from entering. It is a powerful protective ingredient in the charms of most cultures.

GINGER: Eaten before the performance of magic, ginger increases the power of a charm. It is a particularly effective catalyst in love spells and in some Pacific cultures is used by sailors to prevent illness and forestall the approach of bad weather.

GINSENG: The name derives from *jinchen*, meaning "like a man," a reference to the root's shape. Like other herbs noted for their resemblance to parts of the body—from mandrake to John the Conqueror—ginseng is used primarily in sexual and health magic, although it has also become part of rituals to break curses.

GOOFER DUST: A standard ingredient in hoodoo, goofer dust almost always has some graveyard dirt in it, but beyond that, the other ingredients depend on what kind of spell you want to use it in. Dried and ground-up snake heads are another common ingredient. Sometimes lizard heads. Salt and pepper are also typical, especially if the goofer dust is supposed to protect rather than attack.

GRAVEYARD DIRT: Hoodoo spells both protective and offensive use graveyard dirt as a fundamental component. The manner of collection, and the ways in which the dirt is used, dictate the effect of the spell. A hostile spell requires collection of dirt from someone who died badly or who while alive perhaps bore the intended victim ill will. A protective spell might use the dirt from the grave of someone beloved to the practitioner or person to be protected. Graveyard dirt must be paid for by an offering—usually a Mercury dime, which highlights Mercury's role as psychopomp—to the spirit inhabiting the grave from which the dirt is to be dug.

HAWTHORN: Long used in rituals of protection and purification, hawthorn symbolized marriage to the Romans. They also placed it in cribs to protect infants from evil spirits. The Greeks too considered it lucky, but it became identified with witchcraft in Europe and was considered unlucky for that reason—and also perhaps because of the belief that Christ's crown of thorns was made from hawthorn. In the British Isles, it is said that wherever oak, ash, and hawthorn grow together, fairies may be seen.

HAZEL: In Celtic tradition, hazel is a tree of wisdom and inspiration. The branches are commonly used for divining rods or tied into a cross for protection or reconciliation. Hazelnuts are said to bring wisdom and visions.

HEMLOCK: Socrates' downfall, hemlock has the particular property of reversing the power of any mixture to which it is added. It is much more potent in negative magics than positive and a very strong aid to most hexes.

HEMP SEED: Burned as an incense, hemp seed improves scrying and divination and will attract spirit guides. It is also useful in the making of magic candles.

HIBISCUS: Useful as an aphrodisiac and in love spells. Also used to induce dreams and enhance psychic ability and divination.

HOLLY LEAF: A powerful ritual plant, holly wards away misfortune and evil, including lightning. Magical tools and implements made from its wood will be strengthened.

HOPS: Often used in tea to restore balance after the performance of magic.

HOREHOUND: Called the "seed of Horus" by the ancient Egyptians, horehound is a strong protection against sorcery. Crushed and scattered during an exorcism ritual, it improves the prospects for success and can protect the exorcist.

JUNIPER: Used in Mediterranean traditions since prehistoric times, juniper has long associations with protection, exorcism, and (through later association with Jupiter) male sexual potency. A powerfully direct herb, not useful in subtler magics.

LEMONGRASS: A useful aid in the development of psychic powers, lemongrass also has powers in formulas designed to cause problems and bad luck in the target's life.

LICORICE: Used by the Egyptians as an aphrodisiac, licorice root is still a common ingredient in strong and direct love and potency magics.

LILAC: A clarifying and peaceful herb, lilac assists clairvoyance and past-life awareness. In combinations and sachets, it ensures that the positive qualities of the other components outweigh the negative.

LOBELIA: A poison that, like other poisons, must be used with great caution. Lobelia can turn a meddlesome or annoying charm lethal.

LOTUS: Associated with Egyptian magic, and referred to in Greek and Indian traditions as well, the lotus is one of the most powerful gateways to astral awareness and mystical understanding.

MADJET OIL: Known from an inscription on the Temple of Horus at Edfu, this oil was intended to reconstitute the bodies of the dead in the afterlife. Its primary ingredients are cinnamon, myrrh, pine resin, and lemongrass. Historically applied to the statue of the god, it is also useful in various rituals involving contact with the dead.

MANDRAKE ROOT: Because of its humanoid shape, the mandrake root has long been a powerful element in spells of all sorts. Used in alchemical rites to create homunculi, it has also been used in image magic to stand in for the human target. Tea made from the mandrake has enormous visionary power. A whole mandrake root is one of the most powerful apotropaics known to demonology; conversely, because the mandrake is traditionally said to grow beneath gallows, it is an integral part of necromantic and black-magical incantations.

MISTLETOE: Apart from its holiday connection, mistletoe has long been used to protect children from fairies, who cannot bring a changeling child into its presence. When burned, it adds power to exorcism rituals, and it is a useful protective herb when hung about a household.

MOJO: In hoodoo folk magic, a small bag, usually made of flannel, containing a number of different items that are intended to have a magical effect. See p. 134.

MORNING GLORY: Revered by the Aztecs and other Mesoamerican cultures for its powers to both prevent nightmares and induce visionary psychic states, morning glory—despite its toxicity—is widely used in infusions by the more courageous practitioners of herbal magic.

MUGWORT: Popular tradition holds that John the Baptist wore a girdle of mugwort during his forty days in the wilderness, and since then, the herb has been invested with powerful qualities of divination, summoning, and prophecy. When burned with sandalwood or wormwood, it is an important component of scrying rituals, or it can be drunk as tea—usually with honey added as a binding agent—to heighten the power of divinatory rituals.

MULLEIN: Traditionally used as the wick in a sorceror's or witch's oil lamp, mullein has a deep connection with both light and dark magics. In India, it is regarded as the most potent protective herb, and it can be substituted for graveyard dust in hoodoo charms. Various folk divinatory traditions employ mullein to prophesy love and good fortune, as well as to dispel demons.

MYRRH: Cited in the Bible as sacred, and used in purification rituals through the Middle East and Europe, myrrh enhances the power of any incense. The smoke is also used to consecrate holy tools and vessels.

NETTLE: One of the nine sacred herbs of the Anglo-Saxons, nettles are used in various folk-magic traditions to capture a curse and send it back where it came from.

OIL OF ABRAMELIN: This oil is first mentioned in the demonology text *The Sacred Magic of Abramelin the Mage.* It is critical to the protection of the summoner in a demonic ritual and is composed of oil infused with cinnamon, myrrh, and galangal.

PARSLEY: The Greeks associated parsley with death and kept it away from the table, believing it to have sprung from the blood of Archemorus, son of Eurydice, who was killed by a dragon when abandoned by his nurse. Thereafter parsley was considered a funereal plant and was dedicated to Persephone. The Romans, however, saw it as an emblem of good fortune.

ROSEMARY: Versatile and useful in various magical contexts, rosemary promotes healing and purity. Used in charms and spells, it exerts a gentle binding influence. It can also be used to draw elves and fairies. Burned with charcoal, rosemary allows access to hidden knowledge.

RUE: Considered a powerful antimagical herb since Hippocrates and other Greek physicians, rue is used as protection against dark magics and also incorporated into consecration rituals. It is also considered a defense against witchcraft and can give clairvoyance.

SAGE: An ambivalent but very useful herb, sage has long been associated with purification and fortune—both good and bad. Legendary for bringing prosperity and good fortune, sage must be cultivated carefully or its properties will reverse. Tradition holds that a homeowner must never plant sage in his own garden, and that unless sage is mixed in with other herbs, it will bring bad luck instead of good. Native American shamanic rituals began with the "smudging," or purification, of the ritual space by the burning of sage.

SCOTCH BROOM: Also known as broom top, this was a central part of druidic herbal magic. It can be boiled in salt water, and the combination of salt and the herb's own properties will ward off spirits and dispel poltergeists. Thrown into the air, it can raise winds; burned, it can calm them.

SEAWEED: Protection and summoning magic involving sailors, sea voyages, or ocean spirits often employed seaweed. In coastal areas, it is used to summon spirits and conduct séances with the ghosts of drowned sailors.

SPANISH MOSS: In areas where it grows natively, Spanish moss is an important part of rituals to banish poltergeists as well as to bring good fortune to a household. Often local traditions using Spanish moss also employ witch bottles to trap and disarm hostile enchantments.

STAR ANISE: Used in purification rituals and to consecrate and protect holy sites in Buddhist and Shinto traditions, star anise also is known to Western traditions for its power to ward off the evil eye and protect against nightmares. Burned as incense, the seeds increase psychic awareness.

ST. JOHN'S WORT: A druidic sacred herb, St. John's wort repels demons and evil spirits, who cannot abide its smell. Carrying it provides protection against being beguiled by fairies and spirits.

THYME: Burned as an offering and to consecrate temples since the time of the Greeks, thyme is also widely used in protection and cleansing magic. Celtic traditions identify wild thyme as a sign that fairies have blessed a place. Contemporary pagan magic uses it as a smudging agent to purify a space before the undertaking of a spell. Worn as a sachet, it increases psychic sensitivity.

TOBACCO: Spirits from most Native American and Caribbean traditions enjoy offerings of tobacco, and the dried leaves were burned to open spirit channels as well as consecrate a ceremonial space.

VERVAIN: Also known as verbena, or "the witches' herb," vervain is powerful across a wide range of uses. Legend has it that the herb was discovered on Mount Calvary after the Crucifixion, which has meant a long association with healing and protection. The Romans decorated altars with it, and in druidic traditions it was included in lustral water, an ancestor of Christian holy water.

WILLOW: The expression "knock on wood" comes from the practice of knocking on the willow tree to dispel evil, and the tree has an ancient association with rituals of protection, divination, and healing. The bark, burned with sandalwood, attracts spirits, especially if burned outdoors during a waning moon.

YARROW: The flowers dispel negative influence and aid divination, while the twigs of the plant have been used in divination rituals throughout history. Yarrow stalks are the orthodox way to cast the I Ching and have been used in numerous other fortune-telling capacities as well. Also known as devil's nettle, yarrow can be used in summoning magics and divination involving commerce with demons.

YUCCA: Native American rites used a hoop of twisted yucca fibers as a magical gateway. Jumping through the hoop would bring about transformation into animal form. A related magical practice used a smaller ring of yucca, worn on the head, as a permanent talisman enabling the wearer to assume animal form.

APPENDIX B
Names and Attributes of European Demons

There are more demons in the world than we could possibly name in one book, even if we just kept ourselves to the Judeo-Christian tradition. What we've done here is hit the highlights of the demonic legions, going all the way back to the beginning, when old Light-Bearer took a wrong turn out of Heaven. The list is synthesized from quite a few different sources. You can start with the Old Testament and various ancient manuscripts by Kabbalists and Muslim mystics, the most interesting of which is the *Testament of Solomon* (TS), a classic of Jewish pseudepigrapha which dates from way back—around the time Constantine started to Christianize the Roman Empire. One interesting thing about the TS is that it's the first of dozens of texts that characterize Solomon as an arch-magician. And here the Queen of Sheba is characterized as a witch, unlike her presentation in the OT. It's also interesting that the *Quran* refers to the tradition that Solomon built the Temple with the assistance of bound demons: see sura 21, 34, 38.

That's your first introduction to most of the big-name demons. After that, we've concentrated on the medieval and Renaissance demonologists. First and foremost among these is the granddaddy of all things occult, Heinrich Cornelius Agrippa, whose *De occulta philosophia libri tres* blazed the trail that later demonologists would follow. Right after Agrippa comes the *Psuedomonarchia Daemonum* (PD), which first appeared as part of *De Praestigiis Daemonum et Incan-*

tationibus ac Venificiis, a 1563 demonology classic by Agrippa's student Johann Weyer. It was translated into English prior to 1584 by Reginald Scot as part of his *The Discoverie of Witchcraft.* At around the same time, John Dee—advisor to Queen Elizabeth, famed mathematician and navigator—was recording his own experiments in alchemy, demonology, and Enochian ritual magic in *Quinti libri mysteriorum.* Not too long after this appeared the first of many editions of the anonymous *Lemegeton Clavicula Salomonis,* or *Lesser Key of Solomon,* which was cobbled together over the course of centuries, and got a new life among scholars of demonology when Aleister Crowley translated part of it and published it as *The Goetia* in 1904. More recently, you've got Collin de Plancy's *Dictionnaire Infernal,* from 1818, but mostly we like that one for the pictures.

And, here as in everything else, we've relied on Dad's journal to connect some of the dots.

Anyway, from all of this history we've tried to put together a kind of Demons 101 . . . just in case you ever run across one, and we can't get there right away to help out. We've crossed paths with some of these baddies and have seen signs of many others. The rest? Well, when the war really starts, they'll rear their ugly heads. And we'll send them straight back to where they came from.

ABEZITHIBOD: In *The Testament of Solomon* (TS), bound and brought back from the Red Sea by Ephippas to support one of the columns of the Temple. Responsible for the pursuit of the Israelites by the Egyptians:

> *In the exodus of the sons of Israel I hardened the heart of Pharaoh. And I excited his heart and that of his ministers. And I caused them to pursue after the children of Israel. And Pharaoh followed with [me] and all the Egyptians. Then I was present there, and we followed together. And we all came up upon the Red Sea. And it came to pass when the children of Israel had crossed over, the water returned and hid all the host of the Egyptians and all their might.*

AGARES: Odd among demons in that he is often willing to be summoned: "he cometh up mildly," according to *Pseudomonarchia demonum* (PD), appearing as an old man riding a crocodile and carrying a hawk. Can teach languages and "fetch back all that runneth away"— find missing persons? Also can cause earthquakes.

ALLOCER/ALOCER: Described in various texts as appearing like a soldier, riding on a horse, with the face of a red lion and burning eyes. (Yellow eyes? We're checking into it.) According to PD, Allocer "maketh a man woonderfull in astronomie" (which probably means astrology), and will grant knowledge of other sciences as well. Also, he is said to be loud, for whatever that's worth. In our experience, most demons are pretty loud when they want to be.

AMDUSCIAS: Unusual in that he takes the shape of a unicorn until compelled to assume human form. He "easily bringeth to pass, that trumpets and all musical instruments may be heard and not seen, and also that trees shall bend and incline" (PD), in addition to being an excellent procurer of familiars.

AMON: According to PD, Amon appears as a wolf with a serpent's tail, breathing fire—or as a man with dog's teeth and the head of a raven. Will prophesy.

AMY: There are two interesting things about Amy, other than that he appears "in a flame of fier" (PD). Other than the granting of scientific knowledge and your standard demonic familiar-arranging, he is also said to be able to discover the location of "treasures preserved by spirits," and PD goes on to say that Amy retains some of his angelic nature, and "hopeth after a thousand two hundreth yeares to returne to the seventh throne."

ANDRAS: An angel with the head of a raven, riding a black wolf and carrying a sword. A demon of pure murder, "he can kill the master, the servant, and all assistants" (PD).

ANDROALPHUS/ANDREALPHUS: PD cites his appearance as a peacock, and in human form master of "all things belonging to measurements"; in addition, he can change humans into various bird shapes.

ASMODEUS (ASMODAY/SIDONAY/SYDONAY): Proud and arrogant demon. According to TS, even bound, he scorns Solomon: "But how shall I answer thee, for thou art a son of man; whereas I was born an angel's seed by a daughter of man, so that no word of our heavenly kind addressed to the earth-born can be overweening." His star is Ursa Major, also known as the Dragon's Child, and his task on earth is to turn desire into hate: "My business is to plot against the newly wedded, so that they may not know one another. And I sever them utterly by many calamities, and I waste away the beauty of virgin women, and estrange their hearts. . . . I transport men into fits of madness and desire, when they have wives of their own, so that they leave them, and go off by night and day to others that belong to other men; with the result that they commit sin, and fall into murderous deeds." He is subject only to the archangel Raphael, although according to Solomon, the smell of burning fish liver puts him to flight. Asmodeus also hates water.

PD (where he is called Asmoday) differs on appearance and powers: here he has three heads, "whereof the first is like a bull, the second like a man, the third like a ram, he hath a serpents taile, he belcheth flames out of his mouth, he hath feete like a goose, he sitteth on an infernall dragon, he carrieth a lance and a flag in his hand." Under the power of a magic silver ring, and when called by his name, he will teach the sciences and answer all questions truly, including the locations of hidden things.

ASTAROTH: "A foul angel sitting upon an infernal dragon, and carrying in his right hand a viper" (PD). Will prophesy and will tell the story of the demons' fall from grace, although PD says Astaroth will not admit his own part in the fall. A note on his summoning: PD cautions that his breath is poisonous and warns the conjuror to keep his distance and to keep a silver ring near his face.

AYM: Aym rides a snake and carries a torch symbolically understood to be used for the burning of cities. He appears with three heads: one human, one a snake's, and one a cat's. His gifts to the conjuror tend to be private, and true to the snake's Biblical role as facilitator of knowledge; he "maketh one wittie everie kind of waie" (PD), and will give true answers to questions about "privie matters."

BAAL: According to PD, the "first and principal king" of demons, appearing with three heads: one a toad's, one a man's, one a cat's. Can offer the power of invisibility and make men wise. Before assimilation into demonic ranks, was under various names primary deity of numerous Semitic tribes, who sacrificed to him by the burning of their children.

BALAM: According to PD, "Balam is a great and a terrible king, he commeth foorth with three heads, the first of a bull, the second of a man, the third of a ram, he hath a serpents taile, and flaming eies, riding upon a furious [very powerful] beare, and carrieng a hawke on his fist, he speaketh with a hoarse voice, answering perfectlie of things present, past, and to come, hee maketh a man invisible and wise, hee governeth fourtie legions, and was of the order of dominations."

BARBATOS: In PD, he appears in Sagittarius. Understands the languages of animals and birds and can detect things hidden by enchantment. Also sees the future.

BATHIN/BATHYM (MATHIM/MARTHIM): PD describes him as a man with a serpent's tail, riding a horse. Knows herb and gem lore and has the power of "transferring men suddenly from country to country."

BEELZEBOUL: According to the TS, he "has kingship over the demons" and is equated with Satan. His star is Venus (in some sources). Bound by one of his own demons, Ornias, at the command of Solomon, and forced to call each of the other demons in turn so that Solomon might learn more about them. Calls himself "first angel in the first heaven" and says to Solomon:

> I destroy kings. I ally myself with foreign tyrants. And my own demons I set on to men, in order that the latter may believe in them and be lost. And the chosen servants of God, priests and faithful men, I excite unto desires for wicked sins, and evil heresies, and lawless deeds; and they obey me, and I bear them on to destruction. And I inspire men with envy, and murder, and for wars and sodomy, and other evil things. And I will destroy the world.

Can be overpowered, according to TS, by the name Eleéth. Name related to Baal.

BELIAL: According to PD, Belial has the form of an angel. He will offer knowledge if "constrained by divine venue, when he taketh sacrifices, gifts, and offerings," but "he tarrieth not one houre in the truth."

PD also has this to say about Solomon:

> The exorcist must consider, that this Beliall doth in everie thing assist his subjects. If he will not submit himselfe, let the bond of spirits

be read: the spirits chaine is sent for him, wherewith wise Salomon gathered them togither with their legions in a brasen vessell, where were inclosed among all the legions seventie two kings, of whome the cheefe was Bileth, the second was Beliall, the third Asmoday, and above a thousand thousand legions. Without doubt (I must confesse) I learned this of my maister Salomon; but he told me not why he gathered them together, and shut them up so: but I beleeve it was for the pride of this Beliall. Certeine nigromancers doo saie, that Salomon, being on a certeine daie seduced by the craft of a certeine woman, inclined himselfe to praie before the same idoll, Beliall by name: which is not credible. And therefore we must rather thinke (as it is said) that they were gathered together in that great brasen vessell for pride and arrogancie, and throwne into a deepe lake or hole in Babylon. For wise Salomon did accomplish his workes by the divine power, which never forsooke him.

Perhaps an identification of Belial with Moloch here. See TS story of grasshoppers.

BELPHEGOR: Demon of get-rich-quick schemes. Seduces by means of suggesting inventions and discoveries. Associated through this with wealth, and also laziness. According to de Plancy, hell's ambassador to France. Possibly associated with Baal (Baal-peor), in a context of ritualized sex.

BERITH: Given three names in PD: Beall (Baal? Belial?), Berithi, Bolfry. Appears as a crowned red soldier on a red horse. Can only be summoned at a certain hour (note that PD does not specify which), and will prophesy, although he will lie. Has the powers of the alchemist according to PD: "he turneth all metals into gold."

BIFRONS: PD says only that Bifrons appears "in the similitude of a monster." If he can be forced into human form, he will teach astrology, "absolutely declaring the mansions of the planets." Also knows herb and gem lore. Like Bune, he "changeth dead bodies from place to place, he seemeth to light candles upon the sepulchres of the dead."

BILETH/BYLETH: Appears angry when conjured. PD offers specific notes on his conjuration—see notes on conjuration. Primary power is love/seduction: "There is none under the power & dominion of the conjuror, but he that detaineth both men and women in foolish love, till the exorcist hath had his pleasure."

PD is apparently afraid of Bileth: "If any exorcist have the art of Bileth, and cannot make him stand before him, nor see him, I may not disclose how and declare the means to contain him, because it is abomination."

BOTIS: According to PD, appears as either a viper or a human with fangs and horns, carrying a sword. (See TS on unnamed demon who haunts tombs, although Botis is said in PD to prophesy instead of attack people in graveyards.)

BUER: PD says he teaches philosophy and logic, as well as the lore of herbs. Can procure familiars and heal disease.

BUNE: PD notes that Bune "maketh the dead to change their place, and devils to assemble upon the sepulchers." Also grants riches and wisdom. Appears in the form of a three-headed dragon, one of whose head is "like to a man"; compare TS's description of Tribolaios.

CAIM/CAYM: Often appears in the form of a thrush or blackbird, but can take human form, armed with a sword. He "maketh the best disputers" (demon of lawyers, I guess) and can teach "the understanding of all birds, of the lowing of bullocks, and barking of dogs, and also of the sound and noise of waters" (PD).

CIMERIES: Cimeries rides a black horse and rules over Africa, according to canonical demonology (and yeah, we thought of "Conan the Cimmerian," too). But unlike the Barbarian, Cimeries is a bit of a scholar. He will teach "grammar, logicke, and rhetorike" (PD), as well as show the way to hidden treasures. Another thing he's good at, apparently, is moving soldiers up the ranks—in the army, as elsewhere, it pays to be a smooth talker.

DECARABIA (CARABIA): PD notes that Decarabia has power over birds and can grant that power to the conjuror. Also, like many other demons, Decarabia "knoweth the force of herbs and precious stones."

ELIGOR (ABIGOR): Appears as a handsome knight, with lance and scepter. Can be consulted on military strategy "and how soldiers should meet" (PD). Also can prophesy.

ENEPSIGOS: Has a number of shapes (TS), reflecting "abode in the moon." Prophesies to Solomon the destruction of the Temple, after which the bound demons "will go forth in great power hither and thither, and be disseminated all over the world."

EPHIPPAS: Arabian wind demon. In TS, Solomon binds Ephippas at the request of an Arabian king and forces him to lift up and lay the cornerstone of the Temple. Also mentioned, not by name, in the account of Solomon in Sibley's *A New and Complete Illustration of the Occult Sciences* (OS).

FLAUROS: Flauros appears to have very different powers depending on the circumstances of his conjuration. If a triangle is used in the summoning ritual, PD says that he "lieth in all things"; if other symbols are used, Flauros is forced to give true prophecies. He is also, once bound, able to keep the conjuror free of temptation, and will "burne and destroie all the conjurors adversaries." Appears as a leopard until forced to assume human shape, when he is said to have fiery eyes.

FOCALOR: A man with wings of a griffin (PD—often meaning vulture). Another demon with control over the oceans: "He killeth men, and drowneth them in the waters, and overturneth ships of warre, commanding and ruling both winds and seas."

FORAS/FORRAS/FORCAS: Another demon cited by PD as human shaped and granting knowledge of herb and gem lore. Also "teacheth fully logic, ethic, and their parts," as well as invisibility. Can grant long life and recover that which is lost.

FORNEUS (RONOVE/RONEVE): Takes appearance of "a monster of the sea" (PD). Grants knowledge of languages, as well as "adorneth a man with a good name." PD describes Ronove in almost exactly the same terms.

FURCAS: According to PD, "cometh forth in the similitude of a cruel man, with a long beard and a hoary head." Rides a horse and carries a spear. Can teach the sciences and philosophy.

FURFUR: Appears as a stag with a fiery tail. Will lie unless he is summoned within a triangle (PD). Can cause people to fall in love, and can also raise lightning and thunder.

GAAP: When in human form, sometimes appears as a doctor. PD suggests he is one of the most powerful demons; among his other powers, including learning and control of emotions, he also "delivereth familiars out of the possession of other conjurors" and "transferreth men most speedily into other nations."

GAMIGIN/GAMYGYN: PD notes that Gamigin "is seen in the form of a little horse." He "bringeth also to pass, that the souls which are drowned in the sea, or which dwell in Purgatory, shall take airy bodies, and evidently appear" to answer questions if the conjuror wishes.

GLASYA LABOLAS (CAACRINOLAAS/CAASSIMOLAR): PD ascribes a number of abilities: Glasya said to be "captain of murderers" who can prophesy and "gain the minds and love of friends and foes," as well as grant invisibility. Appears as a dog with a griffin's wings.

GOMORY: Takes the appearance of a woman riding a camel. Prophesies about hidden things. Can procure the love of women; in PD, "especially of maids."

GUSOIN: In PD he appears in the form of a Xenophilus. Word appears nowhere else. Meaning unknown.

HAAGENTI: At first, Haagenti must be summoned in the form of a "mighty bull with gryphon's wings" (Lemegeton). Then he must be forced into human shape before the conjuror can make him do anything. Once that's done, though, he is a great alchemist. Will turn metals into gold, and in a debased mimicry of New Testament miracles, can also change water and wine back and forth into each other. Also said to be a "prince of gluttony," according to some Christian mystical traditions.

HALPHAS: According to PD, he "cometh abroad like a stork with a hoarse voice," he "buildeth up towns full of munition and weapons, he sendeth men of war to places appointed." Much the same as Sabnac and Malphas; possible these three are aspects of a single demon, unnamed by PD or in other texts.

IPOS/IPES (AYPOROS/AYPEROS): Notable primarily for PD's odd description: "appearing in the shape of an angel, and yet indeed more obscure and filthy than a lion, with a lion's head, a goose's feet, and a hare's tail." Will prophesy and "maketh a man witty"—Writers? Courtiers?

KOSMOKRATES: A swarm of dangerous demons in TS, attested as follows:

> The first said: "I, O Lord, am called Ruax, and I cause the heads of men to be idle, and I pillage their brows. But let me only hear the words, 'Michael, imprison Ruax,' and at once I retreat."
>
> And the second said: "I am called Barsafael, and I cause those who are subject to my hour to feel the pain of migraine. If only I hear the words, 'Gabriel, imprison Barsafael,' at once I retreat."
>
> The third said: "I am called Arôtosael. I do harm to eyes, and grievously injure them. Only let me hear the words, 'Uriel, imprison Aratosael' (sic), at once I retreat. . . ."
>
> The fifth said: "I am called Iudal, and I bring about a block in the ears and deafness of hearing. If I hear, 'Uruel Iudal,' I at once retreat."
>
> The sixth said: "I am called Sphendonaêl. I cause tumours of the parotid gland, and inflammations of the tonsils, and tetanic recurvation. If I hear, 'Sabrael, imprison Sphendonaêl,' at once I retreat."
>
> And the Seventh said: "I am called Sphandôr, and I weaken the strength of the shoulders, and cause them to tremble; and I paralyze the nerves of the hands, and I break and bruise the bones of the neck.

And I, I suck out the marrow. But if I hear the words, 'Araêl, imprison Sphandôr,' I at once retreat."

And the eighth said: "I am called Belbel. I distort the hearts and minds of men. If I hear the words, 'Araêl, imprison Belbel,' I at once retreat."

And the ninth said: "I am called Kurtaêl. I send colics in the bowels. I induce pains. If I hear the words, 'Iaôth, imprison Kurtaêl,' I at once retreat."

The tenth said: "I am called Metathiax. I cause the reins to ache. If I hear the words, 'Adônaêl, imprison Metathiax,' I at once retreat."

The eleventh said: "I am called Katanikotaêl. I create strife and wrongs in men's homes, and send on them hard temper. If any one would be at peace in his home, let him write on seven leaves of laurel the name of the angel that frustrates me, along with these names: Iae, Ieô, sons of Sabaôth, in the name of the great God let him shut up Katanikotaêl. Then let him wash the laurel-leaves in water, and sprinkle his house with the water, from within to the outside. And at once I retreat."

The twelfth said: "I am called Saphathoraél, and I inspire partisanship in men, and delight in causing them to stumble. If any one will write on paper these names of angels, Iacô, Iealô, Iôelet, Sabaôth, Ithoth, Bae, and having folded it up, wear it round his neck or against his ear, I at once retreat and dissipate the drunken fit."

The thirteenth said: "I am called Bobêl, and I cause nervous illness by my assaults. If I hear the name of the great 'Adonaêl, imprison Bothothêl,' I at once retreat."

The fourteenth said: "I am called Kumeatêl, and I inflict shivering fits and torpor. If only I hear the words: 'Zôrôêl, imprison Kumentaêl,' I at once retreat."

The fifteenth said: "I am called Roêlêd. I cause cold and frost and pain in the stomach. Let me only hear the words: 'Iax, bide not, be not warmed, for Solomon is fairer than eleven fathers,' I at [once] retreat."

The sixteenth said: "I am called Atrax. I inflict upon men fevers, irremediable and harmful. If you would imprison me, chop up coriander and smear it on the lips, reciting the following charm: 'The fever which is from dirt. I exorcise thee by the throne of the most high God, retreat from dirt and retreat from the creature fashioned by God.' And at once I retreat."

The seventeenth said: "I am called Ieropaêl. On the stomach of men I sit, and cause convulsions in the bath and in the road; and wherever I be found, or find a man, I throw him down. But if any one will say to the afflicted into their ear these names, three times over, into the right ear: 'Iudarizê, Sabunê, Denôê,' I at once retreat."

The eighteenth said: "I am called Buldumêch. I separate wife from husband and bring about a grudge between them. If any one write down the names of thy sires, Solomon, on paper and place it in the ante-chamber of his house, I retreat thence. And the legend written shall be as follows: 'The God of Abram, and the God of Isaac, and the God of Jacob commands thee—retire from this house in peace.' And I at once retire."

The nineteenth said: "I am called Naôth, and I take my seat on the knees of men. If any one write on paper: 'Phnunoboêol, depart Nathath, and touch thou not the neck,' I at once retreat."

The twentieth said: "I am called Marderô. I send on men incurable fever. If any write on the leaf of a book: 'Sphênêr, Rafael, retire, drag me not about, flay me not,' and tie it round his neck, I at once retreat."

The twenty-first said: "I am called Alath, and I cause coughing and hard-breathing in children. If any one write on paper: 'Rorêx, do thou pursue Alath,' and fasten it round his neck, I at once retire. . . ."

The twenty-third said: "I am called Nefthada. I cause the reins to ache, and I bring about dysury. If any one write on a plate of tin the words: 'Iathôth, Uruêl, Nephthada,' and fasten it round the loins, I at once retreat."

The twenty-fourth said: "I am called Akton. I cause ribs and lumbic muscles to ache. If one engrave on copper material, taken from a ship which has missed its anchorage, this: 'Marmaraôth, Sabaôth, pursue Akton,' and fasten it round the loin, I at once retreat."

The twenty-fifth said: "I am called Anatreth, and I rend burnings and fevers into the entrails. But if I hear: 'Arara, Charara,' instantly do I retreat."

The twenty-sixth said: "I am called Enenuth. I steal away men's minds, and change their hearts, and make a man toothless. If one write: 'Allazoôl, pursue Enenuth,' and tie the paper round him, I at once retreat."

The twenty-seventh said: "I am called Phêth. I make men consumptive and cause hemorrhagia. If one exorcise me in wine, sweet-smelling and unmixed by the eleventh aeon, and say: 'I exorcise thee by the eleventh aeon to stop, I demand, Phêth (Axiôphêth),' then give it to the patient to drink, and I at once retreat."

The twenty-eighth said: "I am called Harpax, and I send sleeplessness on men. If one write 'Kokphnêdismos,' and bind it round the temples, I at once retire."

The twenty-ninth said: "I am called Anostêr. I engender uterine mania and pains in the bladder. If one powder into pure oil three seeds of laurel and smear it on, saying: 'I exorcise thee, Anostêr. Stop by Marmaraô,' at once I retreat."

The thirtieth said: "I am called Alleborith. If in eating fish one has swallowed a bone, then he must take a bone from the fish and cough, and at once I retreat."

The thirty-first said: "I am called Hephesimireth, and cause lingering disease. If you throw salt, rubbed in the hand, into oil and smear it on the patient, saying: 'Seraphim, Cherubim, help me!' I at once retire."

The thirty-second said: "I am called Ichthion. I paralyze muscles and contuse them. If I hear 'Adonaêth, help!' I at once retire."

The thirty-third said: "I am called Agchoniôn. I lie among swaddling-clothes and in the precipice. And if any one write on fig-leaves 'Lycurgos,' taking away one letter at a time, and write it, reversing the letters, I retire at once. 'Lycurgos, ycurgos, kurgos, yrgos, gos, os.' "

The thirty-fourth said: "I am called Autothith. I cause grudges and fighting. Therefore I am frustrated by Alpha and Omega, if written down."

The thirty-fifth said: "I am called Phthenoth. I cast evil eye on every man. Therefore, the eye much-suffering, if it be drawn. frustrates me."

The thirty-sixth said: "I am called Bianakith. I have a grudge against the body. I lay waste houses, I cause flesh to decay, and all else that is similar. If a man write on the front-door of his house: 'Mêltô, Ardu, Anaath,' I flee from that place."

KUNOSPASTON: Appears as a horse with the tail of a fish, but can change into water (note possible ancestry of backahasten or each uisge legends . . . ? Draugr, too?). Self-identified demon of storms and seasickness, per TS: "I am such a spirit as rounds itself and comes over the expanses of the water of the sea, and I trip up the men who sail thereon. For I round myself into a wave, and transform myself, and then throw myself on ships and come right in on them." Cannot survive more than three days out of water.

LERAIE/LORAY: Takes the likeness of an archer. Putrefies wounds made by arrows.

MALPHAS: Typically seen as a crow, although can be compelled to take human shape. Powers concern building. "He buildeth houses and high towers wonderfully, and quickly bringeth artificers together, he throweth down also the enemy's towers" (PD). Can create familiars.

MARBAS (BARBAS): PD says Marbas appears as a lion but can be forced into human shape (note similarity to TS talking about Rath). Also "changeth men into other shapes" (PD) and can cause and cure disease.

MARCHOSIAS: According to PD, "showeth himself in the shape of a cruel she-wolf with a griffin's wings and a serpent's tail." Can be commanded to fight in a man's shape; tells the truth.

MAVET: Hebrew demon that kills firstborn children.

MORAX (FORAII): A bull. PD: "If he take unto him a man's face, he maketh men wonderful cunning in astronomy, and in all the liberal sciences." Also can grant familiars and knows herb and gem lore.

MURMUR: PD describes him as "appearing in the shape of a soldier, riding on a vulture." Can force souls to appear before the conjuror and answer questions.

NABERIUS/NABERUS: PD gives one alias as Cerberus. Relation to Greek Cerberus unknown, as this demon appears "in the form of a crow" and makes men cunning in language ("rhetorike"), although PD also notes that Naberius "procureth the loss of prelacies and dignities"; another demon that promises the world and leads to ruin. Crow form interesting; must explore possible relationship to crow figures in Native American/Norse mythologies and elsewhere.

OBIZUTH: In TS, appears as a disembodied head, with "disheveled" hair. Has "myriad names and many shapes," so difficult to bind. Strangles newborns (in umbilical cord? Caul?). "I have no work other than the destruction of children, and the making their ears to be deaf, and the working of evil to their eyes, and the binding their mouths with a bond, and the ruin of their minds, and paining of their bodies." Cannot approach a pregnant woman on whom the name of Raphael (whose number is 640) is inscribed. Description recalls Greek legend of the Medusa. In a more traditional demonological sense, description of Obizuth's actions strongly recalls Lilith.

ONOSKELIS: In *The Testament of Solomon*, Onoskelis "had a very pretty shape, and a fair complexion, but her legs were those of a mule." Her testimony: "Oftentimes, however, do I consort with men in the semblance of a woman, and above all with those of a dark skin. For they share my star with me; since they it is who privily or openly worship my star, without knowing that they harm themselves, and but whet my appetite for further mischief." Her star is the full moon.

ORIAS: "Seen as a lion riding on a strong horse, with a serpent's tail, and carrying in his right hand two great serpents hissing" (PD), knows astrology and can sway the targets of the conjuror's ambition to grant "dignities, prelacies, and confirmations."

ORNIAS: In *The Testament of Solomon*, the first demon mentioned. Ornias preyed upon a child laborer working on the building of the Temple, taking half of his food and his pay. Hearing of this, Solomon asked the boy what was wrong. "After we are all released from our work on the Temple of God, after sunset, when I lie down to rest, one of the evil demons comes and takes away from me one half of my pay and one half of my food. Then he also takes hold of my right hand and sucks my thumb. And lo, my soul is oppressed, and so my body waxes thinner every day." The angel Michael gave Solomon a ring, which he was to give the child to throw at the demon and bind him.

This being done, Solomon commands Ornias to reveal his nature. Ornias says:

"Whenever men come to be enamored of women, I metamorphose myself into a comely female; and I take hold of the men in their sleep, and play with them. . . . I am offspring of the archangel Uriel, the power of God."

(Sexual predation recalls succubus, although Ornias is presented as male in gender. Ornias also instructs Solomon in demonic prophecy.)

The story continues. "I ordered Ornias to be brought forward, and said to him: 'Tell me how you know this'; and he answered: 'We demons ascend into the firmament of heaven, and fly about among the stars. And we hear the sentences which go forth upon the souls of men, and forthwith we come, and whether by force of influence, or by fire, or by sword, or by some accident, we veil our act of destruction; and if a man does not die by some untimely disaster or by violence, then we demons transform ourselves in such a way as to appear to men and be worshipped in our human nature.'

"I therefore, having heard this, glorified the Lord God, and again I questioned the demon, saying: 'Tell me how ye can ascend into heaven, being demons, and amidst the stars and holy angels intermingle.' And he answered: 'Just as things are fulfilled in heaven, so also on earth the types of all of them. For there are principalities, authorities, world-rulers, and we demons fly about in the air; and we hear the voices of the heavenly beings, and survey all the powers. And as having no ground on which to alight and rest, we lose strength and fall off like leaves from trees. And men seeing us imagine that the stars are falling from heaven. But it is not really so, O king; but we fall because of our weakness, and because we have nowhere anything to lay hold of; and so we fall down like lightnings in the depth of night and suddenly. And we set cities in flames and fire the fields. For the stars have firm foundations in the heavens like the sun and the moon.' " (TS)

OROBAS: "Orobas is a great prince, he commeth foorth like a horsse, but when he putteth on him a mans idol [image], he talketh of divine vertue, he giveth true answers of things present, past, and to come, and of the divinitie, and of the creation, he deceiveth none, nor suffereth anie to be tempted, he giveth dignities and prelacies, and the favour of freends and foes, and hath rule over twentie legions." (PD)

OZE/OSE: Taking the form of a leopard, Oze can both transform a man's shape and create illusions ("bringeth a man to that madness, that he thinketh himself to be that which he is not"—PD). Control over sanity implied here. A cryptic note at the end of PD's entry on Oze: *Durátque id regnum ad horam*—"makes the kingdom of time endure." Control over time, perhaps? Or over the experience of time? Can slow or accelerate aging?

PAIMON: A man sitting on a dromedary (PD), appearing with "a great cry and roaring." Although Paimon has tremendous knowledge, he will dissemble and must be forced to speak plainly. Can control other people for the conjuror and "prepareth good familiars." A note about his conjuration: "The exorcist must look toward the northwest."

PHOENIX: Although this demon appears in the likeness of his mythological namesake—as a bird with brilliant gold and red feathers—he doesn't have much to do with resurrection. In another Greek resonance, PD warns that Phoenix poses the same dangers as the siren, singing beautifully to distract the summoner from the dangers of the ritual: "Then the exorcist with his companions must beware he give no eare to the melodie, but must by and by bid him put on humane shape," whereupon he will grant the gift of poetry and knowledge of arcane sciences.

PLEIADES: Seven spirits appearing to Solomon in TS: Deception, Strife, Battle, Jealousy, Power, Error, and a seventh identified only as "the worst of all." (Evil spirits also grouped by seven in Testament of Reuben, elsewhere.)

PROCELL: Appears in the shape of an angel and "speaketh very darkly of things hidden"—can control water according to PD.

PRUFLAS (BUFAS): In PD, lives around the Tower of Babylon. Man shaped with the head of a hawk (Horus?). PD says he spreads "discord, war, quarrels, and lies," although PD also notes that Pruflas willingly answers questions.

PURSON: A man with a lion's face (PD), carrying a snake and riding a bear. Accompanied by the sound of trumpets. Can prophesy, change shape, and bring forth familiars.

RABDOS: Appears in the form of a giant hound (TS); previously "a man that wrought many unholy deeds on earth. I was surpassingly learned in letters, and was so mighty that I could hold the stars of heaven back. And many divine works did I prepare." Possibly a source of knowledge if bound? TS corrupt here.

RATH: Takes the form of a lion, although also tells Solomon he is "a spirit quite incapable of being perceived." Makes sick men weaker, but also casts out demons. Bound by the number 644, Hebrew numerological sum of "Emmanuel."

RAUM/RAIM: Shaped as a crow, but in human form "stealeth woonderfully out of the king's house, and carrieth it whether he is assigned, he destroyeth cities, and hath great despite unto dignities" (PD). Like Shax in his thievery.

RESHEF: Name means "pestilence." Sometimes known as Dever, and in that version is one of the ten plagues of Egypt given form. Dad had a theory about the odd "Croatoan" message carved into the tree where the lost colony of Roanoke had been. He thought Croatoan was another name for Reshef, or Dever. We never did have time to clarify why he thought that, and now he's gone.

SALEOS/ZALEOS: *The Goetia* makes note of this demon's peaceable nature, which doesn't really square with PD's description of him as appearing "as a gallant soldier, riding on a crocodile." He is said to have power over affection, and is often used by conjurors who want to magically spiff themselves up for a reluctant lover.

SHAX/SCOX/CHAX: PD describes him as "like unto a stork" (ibis? Thoth?); "he doth marvelously take away the sight, hearing and understanding of any man at the commandment of the conjuror." Will lie unless he is bound in a triangle.

SITRI/SYTRY (BITRU): A "very beautiful" demon (PD) when in human shape, inflames passions and "discloses secrets of women . . . to make them luxuriously naked." Appears first in the shape of a leopard, with griffin's wings.

STOLAS: Appearing as a raven until the summoner forces him into human shape, Stolas is said to give knowledge of mineralogy and plant lore, perfectly "understanding the vertues of herbes and pretious stones" (PD). *The Legemeton* has him as an owl rather than a raven.

SUCAX: Not attested in Weyer or *Legemeton*, but an anonymous fifteenth-century necromancer's manual known as the *Munich Handbook* describes him as appearing as a man with a woman's face, who exerts a particular power to make the conjuror beloved of widows. In addition, he is said to be able to transport the conjuror over long distances (a la the Wild Hunt?) and to teach languages.

TEPHRAS: Appears as a whirlwind under a crescent (horned) moon. "I bring darkness on men, and set fire to fields; and I bring homesteads to naught" (TS). But also heals the "hemitertian fever" (TS—convulsive disorder? Epilepsy?).

TRIBOLAIOS: Appears in TS as "a dragon, three-headed, of fearful hue," though with human hands. Dispelled/controlled by the writing of Golgotha. "I blind children in women's wombs, and twirl their ears round. And I make them deaf and mute. And I have again in my third head means of slipping in. And I smite men in the limbless part of the body, and cause them to fall down, and foam, and grind their teeth." Compare Bune.

VALEFAR (MALEPHAR/MALAPHAR): Takes the form of a lion with a human's (thief's?—PD) head. PD notes with some irony that he "is very familiar with them to whom he maketh himself acquainted, till he hath brought them to the gallows." Another demon that plants ideas of evil in seductive ways.

VAPULA: According to PD, "Vapula is a great duke and a strong, he is seene like a lion with griphens wings, he maketh a man subtill and wonderfull in handicrafts [mechanics], philosophie, and in sciences conteined in bookes, and is ruler over thirtie six legions."

VEPAR (SEPAR): "He is like a mermaid, he is the guide of the waters" (PD), brings storms and shipwrecks. Also, like Sabnac, putrefies wounds.

VINE: In PD, he "showeth himself as a lion, riding on a black horse, and carrying a viper in his hand." Builds and destroys cities and "maketh waters rough." Can also prophesy and—note—"answer of witches."

VOLAC/VALAC: A boy with angel's wings, riding on a two-headed dragon (PD). Has the power to deliver snakes into the conjurors' control.

VUALL/WAL: Once forced out of the camel shape which is his pre-ferred guise, Vuall will prophesy and, according to PD, win for the conjuror the love of "freends and foes," as well as women. There's only one hitch: "he soundeth out in a base [deep] voice the Ægyptian toong."

ZAGAN/ZAGAM: A bull with griffin's wings (PD). Capable of transformations of all metals into "the coin of that dominion," as well as water into wine and vice versa, blood into oil and vice versa.

ZEPAR: Sexual demon, "appearing as a soldier" (PD). Causes passion of women for men and "changeth their shape, until they may enjoy their beloved" (note possible bearing to other shapechanging sexual demons—incubus/succubus—also apocryphal stories of Solomon and Sheba, in which Sheba changed her form to make Solomon desire her). Also makes women barren.

NOW AVAILABLE FROM TITAN BOOKS

Original *Supernatural* novels, revealing all-new Winchester brothers adventures